I0529094

Copyright © 2025 Nathan Smolensky

All rights reserved. No part of this book may be reproduced or used in any manner without the prior written permission of the publisher or copyright owner, except for the use of brief quotations in a book review.

To request permissions, contact UniFire Publications at unifirepublications@gmail.com

ISBN: 979-8-9995638-0-4 (Paperback)

ISBN: 979-8-9995638-1-1 (Hard Cover)

ISBN: 979-8-9995638-2-8 (E-Book)

First edition August 2025

Contents

Introduction

The Case Against Despair

Politics, in its current form, is miserable. We yell and we fight, we sever friendships and relationships, we do whatever we can to make our points heard. And yet, the needle so rarely moves. People rarely move.

A great portion of the problem is that this blusterous style works—or rather, it sells. The divisive rhetoric we hear so often, bandied about by politicians and media, driven by emotional appeals and colored by coded language, preaches above all to its choir. It's effective at building energy in the in-group, generating clicks, reads, donations, and even votes. As for anyone who wasn't already inclined to agree—well, they probably weren't listening anyway.

Where this approach fails profoundly, however, is in the personal. We grow further and further from that aunt we can't understand, or that nephew, or that coworker we used to call a friend. Our tendency toward riling up instead of reaching out leaves us trapped more and more in our ideological bubbles. It's not just that we don't want to talk to those who might deviate from where we stand, it's that we *can't*—we don't share values, we don't agree on the facts, and sometimes it seems like we don't even speak the same language. The more alien we seem to one another, the less we want to listen, and the more we're inclined to view these conflicts in the most extreme terms.

And while the fiery rhetoric might work to get politicians elected, it doesn't lend itself well to lawmakers working together, to governance that is responsive and effective. There is enormous incentive in place for our leaders to play to the theatre and feed the division, to perpetuate our tension rather than to solve our problems. As these leaders fail to lead, our crises worsen, the people's frustration grows, and the rising heat only makes the rabble-rousing more profitable.

All of this leaves us pulling harder and harder in our tug of war. If we could only take a step back and look at all these years of conflict and division in the Social Media Age, we might realize that there is no real winning to be found, but a deepening chaos that offers soil fertile only for corruption, destruction, and exploitation. On the ground, we have millions upon millions of Americans who care deeply about their principles and their vision for our nation, who find themselves more and more alienated, anxious, and afraid, who believe that the Other Side will never listen to them, that it cannot be reasoned with, and that it is bound to be their enemy in war.

But does it really have to be that way?

For the past ten years, I've found myself in the political muck, trying to change things for the better from as far inside as I could go. I ran for office, I served as director of a state party, and I worked in messaging and strategy roles in a range of reform- and depolarization-minded organizations, largely in the independent or third-party space.

To say that these endeavors were entirely successful would be a lie. Like any other aspiring players in the game, we scraped for energy, for attention, for any semblance of perceived momentum we could claim. We catered to our own audience, and at times fell as much into our niche, into our own bubble, as anyone else. And yet, somewhere along that journey, there were flashes of something different, of something better.

The strongest candidates I worked with seemed to have something in common—they *listened*, and they made their constituents feel heard without speaking for them. Despite all the obstacles stacked against them, these candidates were able to capture a new kind of energy, empowering and inspiring in a way no one else could.

Likewise, the greatest breakthroughs in my own conversations came when I stopped trying to win arguments and started to embrace learning from others' perspectives. The more I realized that sharing differing ideas could be a collaborative process rather than a competitive one, the better I was able not only to enjoy the dialogue, but to make others genuinely consider what it was that I had to offer.

The truth is, these ideas are all well understood—outside the political realm. In business and in the sciences, the best strategies and the best solutions have long been found through team members challenging one another, building off one another, and ultimately working together. We assume often that it would be impossible to apply this to politics, but that assumption is dangerous, it is destructive, and it is wrong.

Seeing the success and the impact that a more constructive approach was having, I set about trying to understand the mindsets and frameworks that might allow others to engage in this sort of dialogue. Through these, we can break down our assumptions of how politics has to be, and experience the possibilities of what it can be. **Through these, I believe we can forge a new common ground, defined not by some set of things to agree upon, but by our ability to face everything else.**

This common ground—that is, the discourse we can bring about through a healthier reimagining of politics—can nurture diverse expression and empower voices all across the ideological spectrum. It can make full use of our democratic freedoms of expression, to plant the seeds of a robust crop of ideas and solutions.

Mine is not a plea for civility for the sake of civility. I am not asking any reader to compromise their values, to change their stances, or to abandon their party. I am not here to tell anyone who feels impassioned or enraged that they don't have the right to feel this way—who am I to say they don't? What I *am* here to say is that the same tools that can help us make others feel heard are the very ones that ultimately allow us to be better heard ourselves.

The change we need is not going to come from the top down—our elected governance is by now as much downstream of our politics of division as it is driving it. But if we can show that a healthier approach can work, through better interpersonal discourse, through productive conversations that heal relationships and make us and those around us feel heard and empowered, then this can permeate through the culture and make a real societal impact.

> The common ground we need is defined not by the things we agree upon, but by our ability to face everything else.

The book ahead is divided into five parts. In the first, we'll be assessing the nature, degree, and hazards of our current division, not only to appreciate how pernicious and potent it is, but to realize that it is, ultimately, a finite challenge that we can overcome.

In the second, we'll be challenging our assumptions about political identity, and about what it means fundamentally to think about issues. We'll explore the nature of our conflict mentality when it comes to discourse, how it is both unnecessary and unproductive, and how we can move away from it.

In parts three and four, respectively, I'll be presenting the tools and frameworks to make dialogue more productive, and the ways in which we can apply those to our daily lives and bring others into the conversation. We'll also be looking at the limitations of such approaches, at the obstacles we may face along our way, and at the incredible impacts we can have on those around us if we should succeed.

Finally, we'll break down how better discourse can viably make its way into our electoral arena, and what it would take to challenge institutional power and disrupt cycles of dysfunction and corruption. We'll be exploring what it means to have an ideologically diverse movement of unifiers, and at what kind of dynamic ideas can help us break through the noise and excite people in a way only empowered new voices can.

This book is for anyone who has seen relationships they once held dear strain and suffer because of political differences, who know what it would mean to be able to reach out and break through. It is for those who believe deeply in their values and their causes, and want to do good by better spreading their word. It is for those who are just sick and tired of the madness, struggling to make sense of it all.

Above all, this book is for you. Enjoy.

PART I

Assessing the Blight

YOUR GOAL: Reject Acceptance

Greetings, traveler. I'm Nathan Smolensky, a messaging and communications expert, here to help guide you along a journey to rethinking politics for the better. Throughout this journey, you'll gain powerful tools for breaking out of your bubble, for breaking down barriers in communication to reach those you need to reach, and even for breaking the political mold if you should so choose.

It starts with examining the polarization and strife that permeate our society today—the severity of our division, the dangers that it poses, and whether wanting to come together is enough for us to come together in the current climate. And at the risk of spoiling anything, the division is quite bad, there are a lot of dangers, and no, not really.

Yet if we take the time to analyze these problems, we can begin to see them more and more as ultimately solvable. Yes, our divisions are deep, but they are finite, and understanding where they come from and how they grow can go a long way toward repairing them.

Yes, those divisions can be exploited in a myriad of ways, but identifying the vulnerabilities being targeted and the profits that they offer can allow us to make sense of a great deal of the negative and seemingly irrational behavior we see.

Yes, many of the most intuitive ways of building better discourse and so forth don't work as well as they ought to, but we can take time to understand why these solutions fail and how they can be improved, rather than presuming that nothing is going to work. Many of the problems we'll discuss are cyclical in nature, but this does not mean those cycles are unbreakable—just that they won't fix themselves.

Put in other words, the environment we're in is not a fertile one for healthy conversation or dialogue across divides. It has been riddled, and continues to be riddled, by its share of pests in the form of forces instigating and inflaming division. All this does not mean the earth is barren, or that we should abandon hope for common ground.

> # Rejecting the notion that there is nothing we can do is the first critical step on our journey.

The most important takeaways in this portion are internalization and motivation. Wielding the tools that lay ahead requires no sacrifice of any core beliefs or convictions, but it does demand a fair amount of introspection, some humility, and a willingness to seriously challenge your assumptions and expand your mind. This isn't always going to be easy, and understanding what it is you're working toward can be a crucial motivator along the way.

Above all, I hope that the chapters ahead should dissuade you of the sense of resignation that our discourse and the state of our politics so often inspire. **For as valuable as it may be sometimes to accept the things you cannot change, these are not such things.**

With the right mindset and the right techniques, you *can* enjoy healthy, positive, and productive political conversations with the people in your life who don't share your worldview. You *can* reach out to those who may seem alien to you now, helping to make them feel heard while feeling far more heard yourself. You can even play an active role in fostering healing on a societal level, leveraging the frustration that so many of us share, and the good that can come from different ways of thinking about politics, into practicable competitive advantages in the electoral arena.

Rejecting the notion that there is nothing we can do is the first critical step on a journey filled with learning and growth. I do believe that you will come out of it with a greatened sense of purpose and direction, as well as a heightened ability to advocate your ideas and represent your values, and I thank you for embarking upon it with me.

1

Why Now?

What Isn't and What Never Was

In 1994, the Pew Research Center began what would become a twenty-year study on polarization in the American public. Starting from that watershed year—more on that later—they would reconvene every decade to survey and examine the views of different sides of the aisle on both the issues and on each other. As it turned out, to put it mildly, there was a lot we didn't agree on.

The trends uncovered by Pew and other key research studies paint a picture of recent years marred by deep disagreement, cultural fracturing, and intense political passion. It is not always the simplistic division that we might imagine it to be, and it is not quite like any schism we've seen before, defined as it is by modern technology, modern communication, and modern problems.

Should the very severity of our division compel us to put all of our differences and personal beliefs aside and unite? No, and we're not going to (also, what would we be uniting under? Who would get to decide?). But if we want to become better communicators within our political environment, then it would make sense to start by understanding what exactly that environment is.

Division, by the Numbers

The idea that the U.S. as a nation has been growing more divided isn't particularly new. By the time the Pew Center published its twenty-year study, "Political Polarization in the American Public,"[1] in 2014, the trends in sentiment that they uncovered didn't come as shocking news to most. When it came to stances on the issues, Pew noted, Conservatives and Liberals had been settling more and more into their respective party camps, evaporating what was once a sizeable ideological overlap between Democrats and Republicans.

The trouble, however, extends well beyond a misalignment in policy positions. In that same study, Pew observed a sharp rise among both Democrats and Republicans in unfavorable and strongly unfavorable sentiments toward the other party in the years covered, with the latter more than doubling on both sides between 1994 and 2014—a jump from 16% to 38% of Democrats with "very unfavorable" views of Republicans, and a jump from 17% to 43% among surveyed Republicans thinking in kind. As the study goes on to note,

> *The survey finds that this strong dislike verges on alarm for many. In both political parties, most of those who view the other party very unfavorably say that the other side's policies "are so misguided that they threaten the nation's well-being."*

Then, perhaps most presciently, the study explores the relation of polarization to our personal lives—the places we live, the company we keep, and the values we hold dear—and finds starkly drawn lines, particularly among those who identified as "consistently liberal" or "consistently conservative". On both sides, large numbers of respondents (35% of the consistently liberal, 50% of the consistently conservative) said it was important to them to live in a place where most people shared their views, and even larger numbers (49% and 65%, respectively) said that most of their close friends shared their political views.

All this was in 2014, before the ideological silo-ing of the social media age (and the onset of the Trump era) was fully realized. A later Pew study,[2] run between 2016 and 2022, found growing majorities of both Republicans and Democrats characterizing the other side as immoral, dishonest, unintelligent, and closed-minded. To clarify, these were four different question prompts, but still!

The Splintered Conversation

All this polarization in the culture at large exists both upstream and downstream of polarization in the elected halls of power. Perceived firebrands don't just generate a sharply divided response after they get elected; they're also able to succeed largely because of an already fractured political media ecosystem.

In 1994, back when Pew began its 20-year study—not a coincidence—Newt Gingrich was making headlines in his run for House Speaker, utilizing combative rhetoric and an aggressive media game focused on the conservative talk radio starting to emerge at the time. His strategy worked spectacularly—his GOP won control of Congress for the first time in 40 years, and their annual fundraising nearly doubled over the course of a single election cycle, from $396.9 million in 1992 to over $736 million four years later.[3] By that point, the Democrats had already started emulating these techniques to preach to their own choir, and their fundraising saw similar gains in the same stretch.

> **If we want to become better communicators within our political environment, then it would make sense to start by understanding what exactly that environment is.**

Again, this was all just with the help of partisan talk radio, and the segmenting of news media into ideological camps has come a long way since. Yet another Pew study from early 2020[4] highlighted major schisms between Republicans and Democrats in the news sources they looked toward—roughly two-thirds of "liberal Democrats" said they trusted the New York Times, compared to 10% of "conservative Republicans," with those numbers flipping to 12% and 75%, respectively, when it came to Fox News. All this isn't even to mention some of the even more partisan-coded and controversial sources found on social media, where a majority of Americans nowadays get at least some of their news.[5]

All of this is akin to a societal phenomenon referred to as the death of monoculture—the idea that, since the start of the new millennium and the emergence of so many entertainment options and channels, we're no longer listening to the same things, watching the same things, following the same things, as we once were as a society. The same holds in the political sphere, as the conversation splinters and the bubbles harden. Within each ideological circle, the issues of the day vary wildly, and even the language we use—thanks in part to thought leaders specific to the Left and the Right—can feel unique, creating a sense that we not only see the world differently, but we live in different worlds altogether.

From the consumer's perspective, in the short run, it's easier this way. Surrounding ourselves with those who agree with us brings comfort. Hearing them panic about the things we're worried about, or rejoice about what we might see as positive, assures us that we're not alone. But continually turning to this comfort over time makes the Other Side feel more alien and more frightening, and that fear is all too easy to turn into views, donor dollars, and votes.

This is not to say that the political style and rhetoric that succeeds these days is a grift, some ploy to take advantage of popular passions and sentiments (to be clear, I'm also not assuming or asserting that all of the politicians exercising it are doing so in good faith). Clearly, though, it works, and the more that it works, the more effective it becomes, and the more difficult it becomes to succeed in the political arena with anything else.

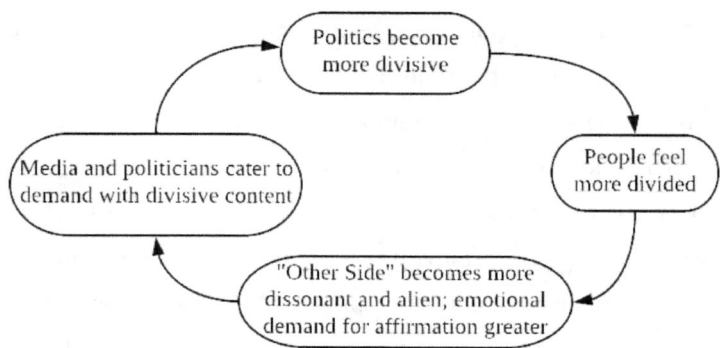

Where this leads us, unfortunately, is closer and closer to a point of irreconcilability. As we lose the ability to have any kind of real conversation, or even to understand the Other Side, we turn to what seems to be the only alternative—entrench ourselves in our respective camps... and prepare to fight.

Losers and Losers in the Culture War

Thus, we find ourselves in a state of perpetual tension, a tug-of-war for political power mirrored by ceaseless yelling on the television and an unease in general society. Friendships collapse, family members disown one another, and every election season seems to create a more panicked state than the one before. The notion of meaningful collaboration and work toward understanding, by and large, has long been forgotten in the political mainstream, and all the relevant players have picked their side and set off rousing their respective rabble.

This is what we often call our Culture War, but the term tends to get a bit confusing. The phenomenon is many things—the heated emotions and contentious discourse around hot-button touchpoints (immigration, abortion, guns, etc.), yes, but also the seeping of politics and political tribalism into seemingly every formerly non-political aspect of life, and even the constant conflict mentality around our discourse at large. All of these elements combine to make for a societal status quo that is unnerving, unrelenting, and, for most of us, quite unfun.

Will it eventually boil over into a more traditional 'hot" conflict? A fair number of Americans seem to think so, with some 50% of respondents to a 2024 Marist poll on the matter saying they thought another Civil War might happen in their lifetime.[6] The logistics would certainly be complicated, with abstract sides not cleanly separated by regional lines and a whole bunch of people who want nothing to do with the fighting. But perhaps even more tellingly, the incentives just don't point that way for any of the key players involved.

Our political ecosystem selects for those who play upon this constant conflict, and as such, it selects for those who keep it going. There is no drive toward resolution, either by escalation (which would have to be exceedingly organized) or de-escalation. Instead, the politics produced by the Culture War are those that leave it in a state of perpetual motion, buoyed by largely performative action and the consistent, looming threat of the Other Side taking power. The media naturally does its part to fuel it as well—again, the unwavering tension gets the eyeballs, the clicks, the subscriptions, and so forth.

Yes, over time, sentiments may shift on certain issues. But this is often due to generational differences and large-scale demographic shift, and rarely due to any "win" in some Culture War battle. By and large, we stay in our ideological camps, and it is unlikely many of the hard-liners would ever waver. What we have, as a result, is a war largely between ideas, where few seem keen on changing their minds, and the regular electoral swings make it difficult to make much lasting progress in any direction.

And if it did somehow escalate? Well, given the chaos and violence that would entail, it would almost certainly lead to tremendous destruction, irreparable harm to the nation and its ability to act on the global stage, and golden opportunities for undermining by enemies and rivals abroad. Victory, by either side, would be pyrrhic at best.

There is, simply put, no winning to be found in this conflict. It would beg the question of what we're fighting for, but another quandary lurks beneath: *how* can we stop?

The Problem Solver's Dilemma

As we look for solutions, whether for our internal division and conflict or for any other societal ill, we look naturally toward our elected leaders. Unfortunately, these leaders have shown themselves ineffective at providing such solutions. What's worse, however, is the reality that doing so would not be in their interests.

In order to reach office and stay in office, ultimately, politicians need to do what works for them. And what works in politics is what wins elections, and what wins elections may not always be what is best for the people.

Money, for one, plays no small part. It's what gets the word out, what allows for mailers and billboards and field operatives running teams of volunteers. Between the 2000 and 2016 elections, the top fundraiser won over 90% of all the races for the U.S. House, and some 80% of those for the U.S. Senate.[7] And while this isn't necessarily causative, it is a strong predictor of success.

Where does the money come from? Well, small donations can certainly add up, if the marketing is strong enough (though the marketing ain't cheap). It is large donations, however, from individuals, corporations, and Political Action Committees that account for the majority of funds raised for almost every U.S. legislative campaign as of 2018[8] (OpenSecrets, which tallied this information, drew the line between large and small at $200). These larger donors, as one might imagine, have many of their own interests in mind, and while a flat quid pro quo would cross some lines, the general understanding is that support is contingent upon favor, and that that favor should be kept.

Another major factor in electoral success is party support, which may not always be monetary. Particularly in races where the general election tends to be non-competitive—which is to say, most of them, as of this writing—having the support of local, state, and national party infrastructure means key endorsements, access to critical donors, and even freedom from new challengers (which parties have been known to throw in when they don't like one of their candidates). In seeking this support, candidates are expected to show allegiance to party bosses and alignment with current directives and talking points, which often leaves little room for their own ideas and expression.

But then, what about solutions? Aren't these the primary service that public servants offer? Shouldn't the quality of these solutions be the thing that we (as the public) select for?

Alas, it's not. Solutions can win elections, but more often for being sellable than for being effective. Drugs are bad, so we should declare war on them. Crime is bad, so we should be hard on it. People deserve nice things, so we should give them those things. Does this always equate to functional policy? No. But it sells.

And so, to any wide-eyed young thinker hoping to offer something better—and there are many out there—the path is precarious. Beyond catering enough to donors to win the election, and beyond aligning enough with the party to stay in its good graces (running without a major party is its own mountain to climb, which we'll get to), there is the challenge of working the ideas through a large legislative body with other concerns and priorities. Any positive outcomes may only follow years down the line, and might not even be clear, depending on the issue at hand—assuming the solutions work at all. If one somehow succeeds, it ends up being *despite* the political ecosystem, not because of it.

It's not impossible. But far more often, we are left with a politics that seems to perpetuate, if not worsen, our problems. Far from this exacerbation being selected away, the empty and divisive political theatre that follows somehow becomes profitable and self-sustaining. And therein lies an even bigger problem.

Patterns of Divergence

In chess, there exists the idea of *maintaining the tension* in a given position, leaving tactical sequences unresolved to create complications for later. It's an effective strategy for pressing an advantage, and on a practical level, it's great for making the opponent lose track and make some mistake. The same idea works in the realm of politics, and—worryingly—it seems to do so exceedingly well.

The tension is what keeps the voters coming back and the donors giving, year after year, election after election. It's the perpetual threat of the Other Side taking power and taking away everything the audience holds dear. It's the perpetuation of the same issues, the same talking points, ad infinitum, with no real effort toward resolution.

In part, this tension is inevitable. America's is a two-party system where power changes hands often, after all. Even if a bold law or reform were to pass, it could simply be reversed by the next Congress or administration. In fact, momentary victories often encourage the opposition to pull harder in the grand tug-of-war we're in.

For the party apparatus, this means turning constantly to the same Culture War issues—guns, abortion, immigration, trans rights, etc. Within our zero-sum paradigm, the parties' brands rely almost entirely on what sets them apart, and the most divisive issues offer the clearest way to gain an edge. These are important issues, of course, but the rhetoric rarely lends itself to real solutions.

Ours is a system optimized for divided times and a broken discourse. It works well to get activists riled up and to spark passion in the energy-driven social media age. And it works to instill the fear of spoilers, allowing the party machines to maintain their preferred status quo.

Such a system is incapable of real compromise. Not only would it be antithetical to the brands of both major parties, it would also make many of the politicians—who fought through primaries by showing how passionately red or blue they are—look like hypocrites, inviting backlash from their valued party bases.

Such a system is also largely incapable of any sort of long-term planning. With power changing hands so often, there isn't the continuity in place to allow for 15- or 20-year infrastructural or environmental initiatives to work, and the rapid election cycles mean little immediate capital is gained for anyone pushing such things.

Most fundamentally, **at a time when our problems are getting more and more complicated, our problem-solving apparatus is getting worse and worse.** The worse our problems get, the more panic and desperation we fall into, leading to even noisier and less effective leadership, which leads to our problems worsening even further, continuing the vicious cycle.

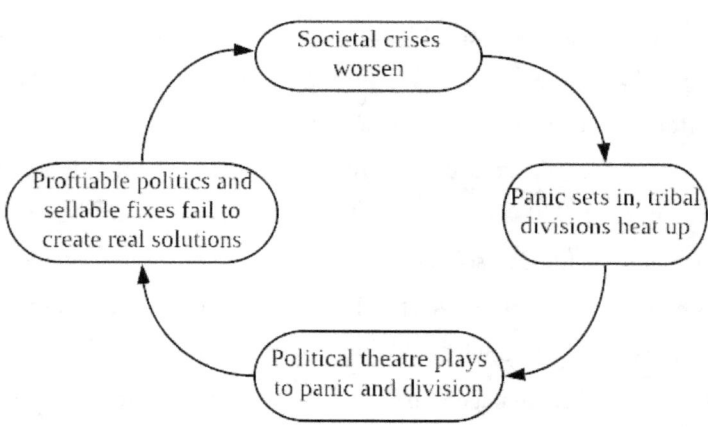

In the best case, this is a cycle of ineffective governance and frustration around unresolved issues. In the worst, it is a spiral, weakening our position on the global stage while we watch the deterioration of our discourse, our politics, and our society.

Uptrends and Swan Dives

A conclusion and a declaration that many will make in my position—that is, the position of someone trying to address polarization—is that the times we live in are the most divided we have ever seen. But as tempting as it might be to say that, I would for several reasons advise against it.

First, as a basis and a justification for action, this is a purely emotional appeal that ends up competing against every other emotional appeal driving political thought. Sure, divisions are bad, most would agree, but plenty of today's crises might be seen as existential—should people really care more about polarization than the wars going on? Than the economy? Than the danger that looms for the values and institutions they care so deeply about?

To many, our division being the worst ever is a line that comes across as just another piece of rhetorical hyperbole, and to that end, it's hard to say it's even definitively true. There is no apples-to-apples comparison to be made between our current schisms and either antebellum America or any other era or place of societal disagreement. Moreover, among the disturbing trends, there are some encouraging signs:

In their excellent 2018 Hidden Tribes report,[9] the group More in Common found that some 77% of those that they surveyed felt that "our differences are not so great that we cannot come together." By their formulations of tribal identity and leaning, 56% of respondents aligned best with "Politically Disengaged," "Moderates," or "Passive Liberals," while only a combined 14% fell into "Progressive Activists" or "Devoted

Conservatives," the factions that seemed to dominate the national discourse and spotlight.

As for general dissatisfaction, well, the politics of the polarization era have been shown to be wildly unpopular in more surveys than one. A 2023 Pew report highlighted that some 65% of Americans "say they always or often feel exhausted when thinking about politics,"[10] while a 2021 project with a more international scope[11] had 85% of U.S. respondents calling for some type of significant political reform.

Clearly, there is widespread frustration with our division, and the demand is there for something different. Finding that something, and making that something *work* within a communications paradigm that favors the loudest and angriest voices, is a different story.

While we wait, we remain volatile, and we remain susceptible to a range of factors that might exacerbate our divisions and tensions. Even when things seem to be trending positively, and even when there are signs of hope, any progress can be easily undone, and new damage may be even harder to reverse.

The most potent instigators of such a thing are the so-called black swan events, named after a book of that title by Nassim Nicholas Taleb. These are dramatic outliers—things that are shocking and unexpected, and that carry high impacts. These are, by definition, not commonplace—a war, a sharp recession, a pandemic, a natural disaster, or some other major geopolitical event—but they do happen.

It is in times of such acute crisis that all of our vulnerabilities are laid bare. Panic sets in, emotions run high, stakes are immediate. It's not easy to maintain collected and rational discourse to begin with, but at these moments it becomes impossible. Soon, demand sets in for swift response and action, and a new cycle of outrage, disconnect, and societal alienation kicks in.

Even in times of relative calm, the way that our polarization interweaves with technology, with social media, and with 21st-century social and political dynamics, creates unprecedented dangers and challenges. Though it isn't necessarily more extreme than any we've seen before, it is unique to our time. And while waiting on historical ebbs and flows to come isn't going to fix everything, some of the problems we face may also, in their own way, be uniquely solvable.

It may well be that we have always largely been in bubbles to some degree, living in our disparate realities, long before our current age of hyperconnectivity put that on display. Communicating and processing information online is new to all of us, and what we are experiencing may largely be, in a historical sense, early shocks.

Moreover, if we can learn to communicate productively in spite of the modern trappings, then we might be able to realize a discourse that is healthier, more empowering, and more democratic than any we have seen before. Of course, that hope is precisely why you and I are here.

---

1. Pew Research Center. "Political Polarization in the American Public." Pew Research Center, Pew Research Center, 12 June 2014

2. Pew Research Center. "As Partisan Hostility Grows, Signs of Frustration with the Two-Party System." Pew Research Center - U.S. Politics & Policy, Pew Research Center, 9 Aug. 2022

3. Mann, Thomas E, and Anthony Corrado. Party Polarization and Campaign Finance. 2014

4. Jurkowitz, Mark, et al. "U.S. Media Polarization and the 2020 Election: A Nation Divided." Pew Research Center, 24 Jan. 2020

5. "Social Media and News Fact Sheet." Pew Research Center's Journalism Project

6. "A Nation Divided" Marist.edu, 2024

7. Koerth, Maggie. "How Money Affects Elections." FiveThirtyEight, ABC News, 10 Sept. 2018

8. The Center for Responsive Politics, et al. "Large versus Small Individual Donations." OpenSecrets

9. "Hidden Tribes of America." Hidden Tribes, 2018

10. Pew Research Center. "Americans' Dismal Views of the Nation's Politics." *Pew Research Center*, 19 Sept. 2023

11. Wike, Richard, et al. "Citizens in Advanced Economies Want Significant Changes to Their Political Systems." Pew Research Center's Global Attitudes Project, 21 Oct. 2021

2

Playing with Fire for Fun and Profit

The Dangers of a Divided Time

"Chaos is a ladder."

It's a line made famous by *Game of Thrones,* uttered by the ever-conniving Littlefinger to explain how he manipulates in pursuit of wealth and power. And even in our real world, it's terribly true.

Today's tensions—our societal distrust of one another, our anxieties around politics and the future, our isolation into ideological bubbles—aren't just things to lament. They can be targeted and exploited by a wide range of actors for all sorts of different profit.

So, who are the Littlefingers making hay of our current division? Well, they're demagogues stirring up angry crowds, foreign agents eager to see us weaken and destabilize, media fearmongers driving views and subscriptions, or even internet trolls just having some bad-natured fun pushing buttons.

Am I going to name names? No, not really, sorry. The truth is, it's impossible to distinguish definitively between willful manipulation on one hand and passionate rhetoric on the other, the latter of which just happens to be divisive and suited to our current ecosystem. I would end up alienating whatever portion of my audience disagrees with my assessment, and to what gain?

Should we fall into a game of pointing fingers, we risk missing the bigger point. Namely, that we have a very sturdy ladder, which rewards and incentivizes the kind of behavior, from individuals, politicians, corporations, media, and more, that we should neither reward nor incentivize.

The Troll Horde and Its Big Red Button

We start with the most relatively innocuous abuse of our divisions, and the one not fueled by any immediate financial motive. Even here, though, the potential for harm is very real.

Online trolling—that is, harassment and antagonizing behavior done for amusement—has been around as long as the internet itself. It's a byproduct of anonymity which pervades almost every forum, and it is worth noting that it probably does its most significant damage outside the political spaces, across teen-filled social media, hyper-popular gaming channels, and so forth.

Unfortunately, the ground of our discourse is extremely fertile for this sort of behavior, and that's telling. Everywhere issues and candidates are discussed, comment threads fill up with name-calling and provocation. Some of the purveyors genuinely get carried away with their emotions, or don't understand how to interact in these spaces. Quite a few, however, know exactly what they're doing.

What drives this latter group? According to *Psychology Today,*[1] traits which define internet trolls include the "Dark Tetrad" of narcissism, Machiavellianism, psychopathy, and sadism, and possibly a splash of good ol' alienation:

*Because loneliness represents a state of chronic frustration
and unmet need, it can trigger aggression toward others
as a way to discharge tension or express oneself—even if in
maladaptive ways.*

To such a soul, the world of online politics offers a giant, convenient red button to feel heard, noticed, and powerful. When emotions run high, it takes only a few choice words to get people raging. Add in partisan animosity toward whomever ends up receiving the brunt of the abuse, and the act might even seem noble.

While this may be something of an extreme case—the chronic and persistent troll, if you will—many more enjoy pressing the buttons from time to time, and it's easier to understand why than you might like to think. After all, who hasn't felt a smidgen of schadenfreude when their least favorite politician blunders or falters, and the stubborn supporters come out in droves to make excuses? Who hasn't been struck by the childlike temptation to tease, name-call, or say, "Told ya so?"

It's hard to fully separate this sort of behavior from well-meaning but ineffective discourse, but where the line is may not ultimately matter. The two phenomena feed off each other, leading many political spaces online to devolve into chaotic, mental-health wastelands.

On occasion, these trolls—or even just the threat of their presence—lead moderators and forum administrators to impose more intense restrictions, from large-scale banning to strict content and language policies. These crackdowns, of course, contribute to even more isolated ideological bubbles, furthering the sense of dissonance, the sense of fear, and the vulnerability to provocation.

All that, largely from a few troublemakers who like knowing they can make things burn. But if they had more motivation, like big money or serious power? Well then, there might be even more serious trouble abrew.

Rousing the Rabble

The troll can do so much harm just for the gratification of eliciting a response. But how much could one do in the pursuit of significant power and capital? How many vulnerabilities could they find and expose in our fractured political ecosystem?

The answer, of course, is a lot.

Deep divisions, tribal loyalties, and a general climate of seemingly perpetual crisis all create strings to pull, opportunities to exploit that Machiavelli could only have dreamt of. For any political operator shrewd enough, making the right connections and telling (a subset of) the people what they want to hear is all too effective a recipe for claiming power.

So how many in the Halls of Power now are profiteering dema-gogues, and how many are largely well-meaning public servants? It's not easy to say, and the lines often blur more than we might like to think. More importantly, again, arguments of who is and isn't a demagogue create a major distraction from a deeper issue at hand.

The system, simply put, is exploitable, and that is a problem in its own right. With a sellable candidate with the right message, and with a whole lot of money to get that message out, power players can prey upon the populace and win election after election. The major parties and power-holders realize that, and they would be fools *not* to play into it. It just works.

It doesn't just work for gaining seats of power. Those who know how to pander and rouse the rabble can also utilize these skills to maintain power, suppress opposition and resistance, and profit in a myriad of ways.

At this point, I would expect roughly half of the readership to be clamoring for me to cite January 6th, 2021, as an example, as a case of inciting violence through rhetoric, and undermining democratic processes in doing so. And I suppose I just did?

I'm not an expert on that matter, however, and I don't expect to move any needles or change any minds with my own take. Even for those who may contend that the story is overblown, though, or that most of the mainstream coverage overlooks key facts, I would argue again that there's a deeper underlying point. If the *potential* exists to incite tribal zealots toward violence, that in itself creates a very, very serious risk.

Behind the strong reaction toward January 6th is something of a fear of fear itself, a fear of a deeply manipulable climate rife for abuse. There is truth in that, and it's not only the politicians themselves who can take advantage of our tribal mentality for their own gain.

Appealing to tribal passions for profit is also an accusation leveraged against many a corporation making a public statement. Advertisements or specials that appeal to either a patriotic, "America first" fervor or to a "woke" sense of political correctness have drawn ire from those who see them as pandering. It may well be that many of these moves are genuine, either as efforts toward inclusion or echoes of certain employee or stakeholder sentiments. But the more general concern remains, that individuals or corporate entities can seek profit or valuable favor by appealing to tribal sentiment—and sowing greater politicization in the process.

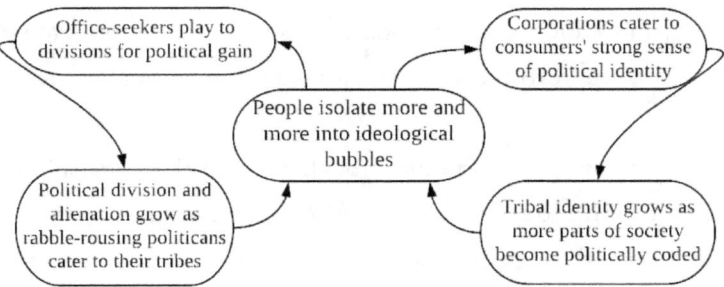

The unifying thread behind all these cases is that of a tribalist team spirit, of a people clamoring to hear what they want to hear. Give them that, and they may give you their vote, they may give you their money, and they may even fight for you. And that's a power rife for abuse.

Taking Aim from Afar

That we are so divided is no secret. The world over, even in places with their own deep troubles, the turmoil and tension in America are well known and carefully watched. If those watching have any unfriendly rivalry with the States, or anything much to gain from furthering or playing upon our division, well, then it would be silly of them not to try.

Here, the exploitation may manifest in a range of ways, from simply propagandizing around the mess we're in, to sowing additional chaos for us to enjoy. When profit can be found simply by furthering the division itself, then all sorts of unsavory options come into play.

The most prominent alleged example of foreign exploitation of our strife is likely that of the 2016 presidential election, after which a slew of articles and exposés were released tying (or attempting to tie) Russian interference to Trump's victory. To many on the Left, the president was seen as a plant, a rabble-rouser positioned by a foreign adversary to take advantage of a gullible populace. To many on the Right, of course, the whole thing was viewed as something of a farce, based on too many overblown connections and fallacious assertions.

It's terribly wishful to think that such an ordeal could lead to much healthy discourse around how we can become less susceptible to deceitful actors in politics and media. What the story became, however, was a cultural touchpoint that deepened divisions and reinforced tribal allegiances. Whatever role Russia or any other malicious actors may have had in this particular case, that ultimate outcome opens a troubling door.

If furthering our divisions is all it takes to weaken our nation's position against rivals and adversaries, and just about any major news moment leads to furthered division, then a whole host of dangerous incentives comes into play. It may be profitable, as the calculations go, to do all sorts of incendiary acts, going as far as to pull us into armed conflict. If we are not only unable to unify, but in fact weakened by each new crisis, then we are showcasing what may be an unprecedented vulnerability, and the possibilities that follow aren't fun to think about.

Even if our adversaries decide to take advantage by simply highlighting our tensions and divisions, the threat may still be, in some sense, existential. Because what underlies any such propaganda, when it gets propagated within an authoritarian state, is an insinuation that free speech and democracy cannot survive in our modern age, and that notion resonates with a great many people.

If our open discourse is only leading to panic and chaos and violence, as these pictures may portray, why *should* people want that? If our embrace of individual liberty leads to easily manipulated masses running amok and hurting each other, that liberty may not be so appealing, and the security of a powerful, controlling authority seems comforting in contrast.

Sadly, there's a kernel of truth in this line of thinking, and it's a big part of why I'm writing this book in the first place. The way that we approach politics and debate, the way that we understand and work through our differences, may well be unsuited to our modern means of communication. By offering better pathways toward more constructive and more productive dialogue, I hope that I might help empower people to make our democracy not only more tenable and democratic, but something that many around the world would hope to emulate.

But we'll get to all that.

Fear Itself (and Those Who Sell It)

None of this fear and division spreads in a vacuum, and it's time to address the channels of mass media that spread it.

It's not anything groundbreaking to say that the media plays a role in spreading fear and loathing through politics, be it through print, radio, podcasts, television, or anywhere else. Two categories, however—cable news titans and social media creators—have received special attention, and these two in particular exemplify the dangerous incentives in play.

Yet again, the problem persists—here, that the media preys upon and exacerbates our divisions—because it works, and the most immediately profitable behaviors tend to rise to the top. With cable and social media, however, the divisive and destructive behaviors aren't just better for the bottom line, but absolutely essential for survival within their respective ecosystems.

In the case of cable news, ratings have been falling for years, as consumers cut cords and turn to (mostly, or at least previously) ad-free, online outlets. But things seem to improve dramatically when viewers have some spectacle to tune into, and worsen when no major crisis is at hand. And so, the drive is natural toward playing up crises or embracing the perpetual crises of our Culture War era, lest the channels and companies behind them run the risk of eventual collapse.

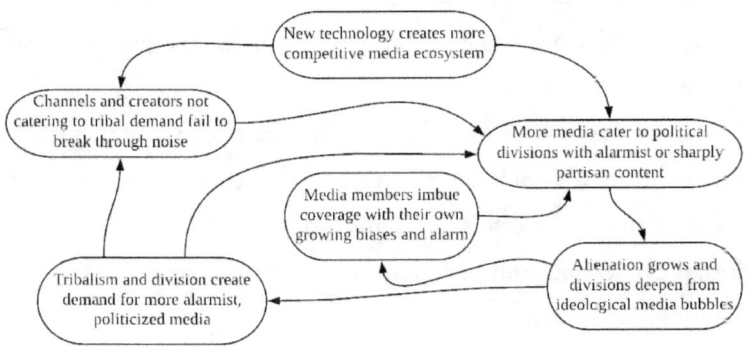

When it comes to social media creators, meanwhile, there may not be as much infrastructure invested, but there is a nearly infinite field of competitors, and the easiest way to break through the noise seems to be with a whole lot of noise. For years now, many of the same online firebrands who've drawn disgust and alarm from observers are those who've earned the most views and dollars from their work, and it's no coincidence. When everyone is fighting to share the microphone, it is the loudest, most charged, most extreme voices that tend to rise to the top.

Now, many of these creators may believe genuinely in what they're saying, and indeed, the same can be said of many who make cable news what it is. How would they expect people to tune in if they didn't help to facilitate a sense of urgency? And how could they create content so effectively if not for some personal passion for what they're covering?

I certainly wouldn't be writing this if I didn't feel a fair sense of alarm around the state of things myself, and neither I nor anyone else is immune to getting carried away. I try to be cognizant of the impact of my words, and on their ultimate ability to unify rather than inflame, precisely because I understand that good intentions in this regard are not enough. Many of those who call attention to fearmongering—whether they come from the Left, the Right, or the Center—themselves point fingers just as sharply, and contribute to the problem every bit as much as the objects of their criticism.

The problem isn't simply that such behavior exists, but that it works as well as it does. Even when the media product it creates doesn't feel like fear, even when it offers the comfort of the only sane voice in a mad world, it can leave us trapped ever further in our bubbles, and less able to communicate outside of them.

The Tragic Madness of It All

Before we delve further into the myriad ways to exploit our divisions, it is worth taking a moment to highlight those individuals who are most preyed upon when they get exploited, by those who suffer most and most immediately from our alienation.

For years, I had a joke I would run out at events, something akin to, "When it gets to a point when you'd have to be crazy to want to get involved with politics, who do you think is going to get involved with politics?"

Over time, however, I came to realize that a very serious problem underlay that observation.

When we stop to analyze the impacts, we can realize that those individuals with some psychological issue or issue—traumas, disorders, or simply a lack of ability to maintain rational thought in more heated environments—are going to particularly struggle with our current discourse. They are more likely to have trouble processing rhetoric with any grain of salt, and less likely to control the emotional response that follows.

These individuals are not only the ones most likely to get swept up in media alarmism or pandering demagoguery. They also tend to propagate divisions through their heated approach to dialogue and, on occasion, through extreme actions.

Most often, these individuals end up being among the loudest voices on various social media forums. These are the ones with tweet counts in the hundreds of thousands, who post constantly and seem to engage in verbal spats in every comment and reply section.

This outspokenness and penchant for drama also happens to be a recipe for popularity in the social media age, and certainly one for attention. To allies and kindred spirits, these voices may come across as raw expressions of a shared sentiment, or as good-natured fun. To the Other Side, they may seem hostile, and the likely response is one of either ridicule or deep concern.

Either way, the flames get fanned, and the emotions involved further deepen. The same troubled souls remain at the center of it, the likeliest to take things too far and push others further apart in doing so.

Deepfakes and Sparks to Come

The criticality of our problem lies not only in divisions growing or word spreading on how to exploit them, but also in new means of exploitation emerging. There's one such tool for destruction that's received quite a bit of recent attention at the time of this writing, and I'd like to take a moment to look at it here.

Deepfakes are images, videos, and audio manipulated through AI to depict, well, fake things, and rather convincingly. It could be a sound-bite that was never spoken, an interview entirely embellished, or even an assassination that didn't really happen. Needless to say, the political applications are abundant, and many are quite disturbing.

For many, a nightmare scenario consists of some particularly compelling piece of deepfake media spreading during a volatile time. Before facts can be straightened, widespread panic ensues. Perhaps it throws the result of an important election, or perhaps it drives some emotional respondents to extreme acts, turning a manufactured crisis quickly into a very real one.

But the threat of such a thing, as understandably concerning as it may be, is yet another realization of the danger of our political-emotional state. As long as tensions run high, our ability to respond with reason and patience to any kind of alarm is going to be severely limited. The volatility will be there, and what comes with it is great danger.

So, what can be helped? Can we really stay ahead of every potentially incendiary event? Or, does the real solution lie in navigating out of the powder keg, of trying to foster a healthy discourse that improves our understanding and lessens our fear of one another? Perhaps, if we can help to build such a thing, we might be able to build up some patience and resilience to manipulation, and all those myriad vulnerabilities may not be so much to worry about.

Which brings us to the hard part.

---

1. "What Makes Internet Trolls Tick?" Psychology Today, 2019

3

Bubble Trouble

A Closer Look at Discourse in Decline

I 'm far from the first to point to division and polarization as a problem, to remark on the damage it has done or has the potential to do, or to try to offer some way to help.

At the time of this writing, a great many voices can be found calling for us to bridge our divides, to stop focusing so much on our differences, and to come together as a nation. Alas, it's not quite so simple.

Yes, we choose often to spend time in our bubbles and to surround ourselves with the like-minded, and yes, this is part of the trouble. But the underlying problems have progressed, and we are at a point now where many are simply incapable of reaching out beyond their bubble, even if they do try. The gaps in worldview, in priorities and perceptions of what matters, even in language, are just too large to easily overcome.

This is our lack of common ground. **It is not simply that we disagree; it is that we lack the mechanism to work through that disagreement in any kind of healthy or productive manner.** Without it, debate doesn't get anywhere, pleas for understanding don't get anywhere, and even well-resourced bridge-building efforts may falter.

Should we want to rebuild some semblance of unity, we need first to take a hard look at what hasn't worked, why it hasn't worked, and just how difficult it is in this age to break through our bubbles.

Argument's Sake

Years ago, when I was a student myself, I had the displeasure of seeing intercollegiate debate up close. It was extremely fast, occasionally loud, and filled with a whole bunch of arguments being tossed back and forth—some, admittedly, quite clever.

Unfortunately, like most debate nowadays, it didn't actually change minds or seriously try to. It didn't lead to real growth or understanding among the participants—takeaways from any given night were typically limited to cool ways to refute a particular line. It was sport, and it was performative, but at least the collegiate version seemed like fun.

Ideally, debate should be about bringing voices together. It is a democratic institution as old as democracy itself, its origins going back to the ancient Greeks and their legendary battles of wits. Whereas theirs, however, was a spirited contest between ideas, or at least aspired to be, what we have today is something altogether different, something emptier.

At the top level, where the stakes are highest, debate purports to play for an audience of neutral or undecided observers. But it's rarely the points being made that sway anyone.

Rather, most analysis following a prominent debate will focus on who made a gaffe, who clocked in the most interruptions and the most words per minute, who stuttered, and who wore what. The exercise is theatrical, and the performances are measured as any actors' would be.

> The problem is not just that we disagree—it is that we lack the mechanism to work through that disagreement in any kind of healthy or productive manner.

What's more, much of the swaying that does occur doesn't come in the form of a would-be voter for Candidate A turning to Candidate B, but from someone with a clear leaning one way or the other being inspired to vote—or not to. To understand this is to realize that the best strategy is again simply to preach to the choir and seek to energize, to gear messages toward firing up the base rather than wasting time trying to change minds.

At the amateur level, when no neutral observers are watching, the results aren't much more promising. All too often, we approach these encounters with the same competitive mindset, holding plans for some elegant refutation, only to have our combativeness met with defensiveness and hostility. A few unfortunately enjoy this sport, but even those looking to genuinely persuade often find their efforts fruitless and frustrating.

However diverse the participants, the act of having an argument seldom brings us closer in the current day and age. Instead, it reinforces the notion that we live in different realities, that we can never get along. And if this is the feeling we're left with, then the clearest courses of action would be either to embrace the sport of it, or to retreat back to the peace and comfort of our bubbles.

Screaming Into the Void (Or Worse)

Alright, let's say we don't want to fight anymore, but we recognize the importance of getting people to come to our side. Let's say we make an overture, and let's say we make it civil and respectful. Surely, they'll listen, right? Right?

During every election season and every heated political moment, there arrives a cavalcade of posts on my social media from friends Left, Right, and Center imploring the Other Side(s) to see the error in their ways. They are impassioned pleas, often quite long, and occasionally well-written. Unfortunately, unless their posters were hoping for a flame war to spring up in the comments (as it inevitably does), they rarely have the intended effect.

These diatribes, after all, are built largely on coded language. Whether it's a diehard conservative warning of the dangers of illegals, or a bleeding-heart lefty mourning democratic institutions under Trump, these sentiments end up preaching to the choir because, frankly, that's the only kind of political messaging most of us know. It doesn't help that many of these messengers are among the most entrenched in their tribes—that's to be expected, since they're the most active online, and most others would be reticent to post such things.

Most of this outreach goes ignored, lost in the noise of common discourse. Some may even backfire, particularly when someone famous is at the helm. In the latter case, backlash and resentment may follow, with voters and tribes energized in a way entirely not intended.

The most prominent of these cases involve celebrities with liberal sensibilities issuing endorsements or appealing to the public to support a particular cause. These are often carefully written, delivered by good-looking artists with years of experience speaking to the masses. But the more left-leaning members of the fanbase were likely aligned anyway, the Middle isn't all that concerned, and the Right often takes the message as some elitist trying to tell them what to do.

You may like these celebrities or hate them (or neither), but if we zoom out a bit, we may find something rather sad about people trying to use their platform to reach a wider audience, only to find themselves incapable of effectively communicating with it. This, unfortunately, is the reality of life and discourse without common ground.

To their credit, a few of these prominent individuals with failed forays into the forum have seemingly learned from their experiences and put time and energy into supporting bridge-building efforts. But even these, no matter how well-intentioned or well-funded, end up facing an uphill battle.

Marketing Against the Madness

Before we dive into the challenges facing common ground-building, dialogue-improving, or anti-polarization efforts, we need to realize that delivering any idea to a wide audience (or any audience) is a challenge of marketing. Marketing has a science, and that science may help us analyze the problem here.

The journey begins with the so-called four P's of marketing: product, price, place, and promotion. To understand these elements is to understand how any core competency or initial idea can reach its intended target, what knobs and levers we have at our disposal to turn, and what challenges we're likely to encounter along the way.

The product, in this context, is whatever it is we're trying to build. It could be a membership organization looking to foster healthier dialogue. It could be a TV special featuring conversations with Americans of different stripes. It could be a candidate or a party. Thinking just of what something *could* be is a wonderful way to feel optimistic—why shouldn't it work? Wouldn't it be so cool if it did?

Now, let's say we start looking at the question of place or distribution. On the surface, we may still fail to set off any alarm bells, because the distribution channels for these ideas are the same as for any similar partisan venture or organization—websites and event spaces, podcasts and YouTube channels and journals for the media efforts. So what's the issue?

> ## Delivering any political idea to a wide audience is a challenge of marketing, and the science of marketing can help us understand the problems we run into.

The trouble is, regardless of where you put these bubble-breaking, conversation-friendly spaces, people have to know where to find them, and they have to want to look. For all the general interest in better politics and better discourse and fresh, more positive ideas, there are only so many people actively spending time and energy in search of them.

As a result, fledgling efforts in the bridge-building space may lack the critical mass needed to build momentum, and will struggle, in particular, to bring in those who need the healthy discourse most. Some may end up experiencing a degree of audience capture as their niche following starts to steer their voice into something less open-minded and pluralistic than what they might have hoped. Those that start slowly may see interest dissipate as momentum stammers. While all this can be counteracted to a degree with initial investment and public rollout, such things can only go so far in a crowded and noisy landscape, and the scale needed to make a difference isn't easy to reach.

Similar issues arise with the promotion of political efforts. Paid promotion, from billboards to online ads to placement in whatever journals, can be intensely cost-prohibitive, particularly if the goal is to reach a broad and ideologically diverse audience. The needed fundraising is even more elusive when the product isn't proven, and the reticence of many to invest in underdog efforts—making them bigger underdogs as a result—creates yet another vicious feedback loop.

If the intended promotion style is unpaid, relying on social media and word of mouth, there is, again, the trouble that these channels favor the most polarized voices. It's the zealots, after all, who most eagerly post and re-post and engage with content. Even with a concerted effort to regularly deliver messages across social media, if the messages aren't fiery and emotional and exciting the way the diehards' are, then they aren't going to spread nearly as well.

And if the hope is for a boost from earned media, then once again trouble stands ahead. Even if we assume the best of faith from mass media channels, it would be a fair assessment to say that there isn't anything worth reporting on if no momentum has been built, or if the potential for success has yet to be demonstrated. What follows from this perfectly logical reasoning is another feedback loop that heightens barriers to entry and advantages the established players in our political game.

I skipped over the question of price earlier, but it does apply to many of these efforts in the form of opportunity cost. Even if they're ostensibly free for members to take part in, the sacrifice of time, energy, and attention required can end up being enormous.

To spend so much on a depolarization effort, and particularly on an unproven one, is an enormous ask for anyone preoccupied with what they perceive as existential or critical issues elsewhere in our politics. It's also a tough ask for anyone averse to politics, to put themselves at the fore of something new and immerse so deeply in discourse.

All of these hurdles don't just inhibit startups and new voices. They also affect those already present, constantly adjusting the equations of what it takes to succeed and sustain in a changing landscape of political communication.

The Kumbaya Conundrum

If you're wondering why I haven't named a whole lot of names when it comes to organizational efforts at depolarization, the reason is largely because I don't intend to speak ill or discourage them. These are promising and noble groups trying to better our society, and I've been a part of a number of them myself—in fact, I might still be a member of one or two.

Ultimately, however, it is worth observing that these kinds of endeavors are going to be limited. They are limited by the brutal competitive environment of modern politics, by a communications paradigm that, by its nature, favors louder and brasher and more divisive voices. And they are limited too often by opt-in models which fail to reach the most critical audiences.

Yes, we can be civil with each other if we choose to be civil with each other, if we make a deliberate effort to be civil with each other in spite of our differences. Other than making a few participants feel good, though, what exactly does this accomplish? What does it prove?

More importantly, when it comes to passionate partisans worried about the lives at stake in the issues of our time, who are we to ask them to be polite? Who are we to ask them to take time away from their activism to spend on some hand-holding that may not ultimately lead anywhere?

Where we end up, if we're not careful, is with new bubbles being formed in these depolarization spaces. We may cheer and sing our songs, but if we don't move the needle, we don't really get anywhere. **If we're not able to apply that civil conversation to those outside the spaces we create, then we're every bit as isolated as anyone else.**

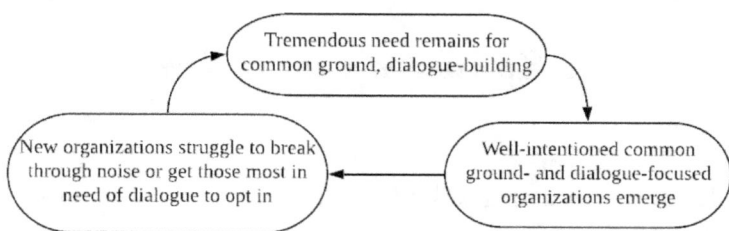

I will reiterate once more that I do not mean to denigrate or discourage any of these efforts. I dedicated years of my life to cross-partisan dialogue initiatives, to cross-partisan and bipartisan and trans-partisan and non-partisan campaigns (yes, all of these are actual things), to party building in hopes of breaking the Democratic and Republican duopoly and the red-against-blue paradigm that comes with it. These have been valuable experiences, and not only because of the moments of hope and promise or the wonderful people I met along the way.

It is through being a part of all of those, through seeing the successes as well as the failures of these attempts, that I came to learn so much of what I understand now. It is through these experiences that I came to realize that the greatest promise may lie in promoting a collaborative and analytical problem-solving approach, utilizing tools for healthy conversation that were first developed for use in non-political fields. It is through that, and through working with many former colleagues from these efforts, that I was able to better understand how to break out of my own bubbles, and how to empower others to do the same.

PART II

Tilling the Soil

YOUR GOAL: Break Free

So, what now? For all that we may lament how various actors might take advantage of our divisions, or how hard it may be to work through those divisions, what can be done? The passions with which we carry our beliefs, the ways in which those beliefs color the media we consume and the relationships in our lives we choose to maintain or discard—isn't that just how politics is?

Well, for many of us, yes. These are the realities of our current times. But this doesn't mean they have to be.

Much of how we conceive politics is grounded in our underlying assumptions, foundations which don't seem as sturdy when we properly call them to question. We assume, when people aren't hearing us, that our only recourse is to be louder and to fight harder. We assume, when others lack our moral sensibilities, that they are incapable of understanding our concerns. We assume, above all, that conflict is the only pathway toward resolution.

It's not. In the worlds of business and natural science, a collaborative problem-solving approach is not only possible, but well understood to be necessary for achieving the best results. We can foster this mindset in our approach to politics as well, and it starts with taking the time to understand why it is we believe what we believe as strongly as we believe it, and how we can *effectively* share those views with others around us. **Only then can we break free from our assumptions around what politics has to be, and embrace the possibilities of what it can.**

I will not ask you to let go of your political identity, to change sides, or to soften any of your stances. I will not ask you to compromise any values. What I will ask, however, is that you consider the frameworks through which you understand and process these things.

> # By breaking free from our assumptions of what politics has to be, we can embrace the possibilities of what it can be.

By challenging our notions of our political identity, of how we understand issues and how we view conversation and disagreement, we can lay the roots for both better conversation and clearer expression of our selves. Through sharing that mindset with others, we can heal relationships and even pave the way for greater democratic engagement in our communities. Friendships can grow. Ideas can blossom. And the lush scape possible upon our common ground can begin to come into view.

4

Heart and Horseshoe

Political Identity in the Age of Ill Communication

I n 1951, social philosopher Eric Hoffer released *The True Believer: Thoughts on the Nature of Mass Movements*, an exploration into the history of ideological movements, the defining traits of their followers, and their ultimate impacts upon both those involved and the surrounding society. With an understandable emphasis (given the time of writing) on the rise of fascism in Germany, Hoffer concludes commonality in both methodology and audience for radical and reactionary movements, and postulates that the same energy can also be channeled toward positive endeavors. The book has since been the subject of a great deal of debate, but it remains a seminal work in the subgenre of exploring what draws us toward fanaticism, and what we can learn from it.

When looking upon the works of Hoffer or anything else in this vein, however, I would encourage readers not to look upon these studies with too great a sense of distance, or with the presumption that any of us is so above it all. Particularly in an age with so many mass movements trying to break through, where our fervor is constantly inflamed by both our political reality and the filters with which we view it, the lines separating the justifiably impassioned from the fanatical are both blurred and highly subjective.

Ultimately, we are all informed by our beliefs, and most all of us would want to do the greatest societal good with our personal perspectives in mind. If this is our goal, then it behooves us to examine the political behaviors of ourselves and those around us with both an analytical and empathetic lens, working to understand why it is our beliefs manifest as they do, how our views evolve over time, and where all of us may be susceptible to going too far.

Politics as Sport

The primary colors of our major parties—the bright red and blue—haven't actually been around all that long. As recently as 1984, *Time* was writing about Reagan's "sea of blue" on the electoral map,[1] with Democratic candidate Mondale securing only "little islands of red." Which side got which was an editor's and a mapmaker's choice, nothing of real significance.

Now, of course, the associations are ubiquitous and iconic. Partisans wear these colors, live by these colors, *bleed* these colors. They're the team colors, after all.

How do we pick our teams? Well, a great many of us follow in supporting the teams that our parents rooted for long before us.[2] Others pick their teams through the values they develop as adolescents and adults, the ideas and speakers that inspire them, and the critical issues that speak to their soul. Whatever the case, the initial connection to one's team tends to be emotional, borne either from formative years and experiences or life-altering introspection. Once we're in, as a result, we're often in deep.

One of the primary draws of sports fandom, according to *Psychology Today,*[3] is a sense of belonging and community, and the same appeal can be found in tribal politics. These are passionate supporters who cheer and celebrate together when they win, who cry and comfort one another when they lose.

This mentality is perfectly suited to embrace—and be embraced by—the current political media environment. Morning talk shows become something akin to sports radio fan stations, dissecting every election and political battle with a relentless energy, a whole lot of noise, and a fair bit of bias.

Implicit within the team mindset is the idea that one should not ever switch teams, that one should be ever loyal. Those who view politics this way are going to be more inclined to vote consistently along party lines, as the success of the party is far more important than the particulars of any one candidate.

Moreover, the party represents a set of essential values, a part of its partisans' identity. It is nigh impossible for even the strongest opposing candidate to overcome that connection, and it is hard to let go of even the most fundamentally flawed champion when they're a part of the team. We put up with them as we do with troublemakers in sports, problem children whose misbehavior simply doesn't worry us as much as it would if they wore different colors.

When the team fails, the fans will be upset. They will often be angry, and may indeed be critical toward their own leadership and players, but any such criticism is nestled in the assumption that the team is ultimately right, and that it would be successful if the world were just and sensible. Given all that, these adherents may struggle at times to see the bigger picture, or to get their message through to those who might not share these assumptions.

Of course, every sport has its diehards, the hooligans who take it too far. The sport of politics is no exception, but to take it even more seriously with such matters is to treat it as something else entirely.

Politics as Religion

To call the most ardent participants of our discourse are zealots is not meant to be any kind of exaggeration. Their relationship with the candidates and issues of the day is interwoven deeply with the core of their beliefs and their identity, and, indeed, it is quite helpful to understand this as a religion.

In reality, the distinction between this and the previous category is something of a blur, but the clearest dividing line I can offer, between a sports mentality of politics and a religious one, is how it reflects and affects the beholder's sense of self-worth. One who treats politics as sport may well see their side as morally superior—indeed, this is common even among casual observers—but it is another thing to see politics as defining one's morality, as the reason someone is a good person.

Here, the entire political arena can be viewed as a battlefield of Good and Evil, Right and Wrong. It becomes difficult to see opinions as opinions, or to regard beliefs as anything subjective. There is only the Truth and the rest, and to not fight for the former would be a sin.

That this level of engagement has become more common in recent decades is an outcome, to an extent, of our bubbling as a society and the feedback loops which accompany it, and to the natural isolation of the driving movements—religious conservatism focusing largely in rural communities, while left-wing sentiment is strongest largely in its academic and activist circles. The trend, however, may also reflect a greater need felt by many for fulfillment, for something to believe in in a world gone mad. In the face of despair and senseless injustice—whether these are real or perceived phenomena—the search for a guiding light of hope is both natural and deeply emotional.

All of this is not to say that those with such a mentality are somehow wrong in their beliefs. If you count yourself among this group, this goes for you—you may well be right, and I'm not likely to convince you otherwise. It is worth lamenting, however, that this religious adherence to ideological thought does not lend itself well to dialogue, let alone any kind of constructive problem-solving.

No, while competing sports teams may have their games, competing religions have historically approached conflict in a far less playful manner, which often carries dire consequence.

Horseshoes and Hand Grenades

Whatever your opinions may be on thought leaders being cynical or conniving, the reality is that many millions of their followers genuinely care and, in their minds, want to do the right thing. But what if they care too much?

At some point, when the conflict becomes one of Good against Evil, and the stakes are life and death, everything and anything becomes justified. However well-intentioned the initial sentiment, what follows this outlook is both frightening and, to its actors, perfectly logical.

There are three dangerous sources adding fuel to these brewing fires. First, there is the sense of importance, this perception of the stakes as absolute. It arises naturally from any impassioned approach, from the relationships we form with our politics and the way we interweave our egos and sense of worth, and from the feedback loops and confirmation biases which grow from our modern ideological bubbles.

The second incendiary ingredient is a sense of absolute certainty, a lack of doubt or hesitation when one comes to conclusions. This, too, is often borne of ideological isolation, and made easier when we allow the most extreme voices to color our perception of the Other Side, leading us to determine Them to be without reason.

There is a third element, however, which tends dangerously to heighten our passion, and it is the idea that waiting and hoping for the politicians to handle the conflict is pointless, and we must take matters into our own hands. While some may attribute this impatience at least in part to our love of instant gratification in the digital age, we should not discount the role played by ineffective and often unresponsive governance. **Every failure of our leaders to make their constituents heard reinforces the notion that they simply aren't listening**, that they cannot be relied upon to do the good that needs to get done. As our problem-solving apparatus is pulled ever more away from actually solving our problems, this has been an especially active catalyst.

Combine these factors—the growing sentiments that the stakes are absolute, that there is no doubt or need for hesitation, and that the politicians aren't going to solve the problems—and you have a recipe for disaster, no matter the source. It is a realization of some part of horseshoe theory, the assertion that the far left and far right begin to closely resemble one another after a certain point. So many of their conclusions are similar—rebellion and revolution, elimination of their dangerous enemies, and a strong authoritarian presence to effectively build and enforce the needed future.

We have not devolved yet into the worst of things, but we have, over these past decades, seen more and more justified in the name of political dogma. I would close this section out by citing two particular examples—the growth in popularity of de-platforming on the Left, and of book banning on the Right.

Critics toward the middle and respective Other Sides see the rises of these as reflective of how we see free speech. In essence, they view these movements as reflective of a change in what means we are comfortable with to reach our desired ends.

> At some point, when the conflict becomes one of Good against Evil, and the stakes are life and death, everything and anything becomes justified. However well-intentioned the initial sentiment, what follows this outlook is both frightening and, to its actors, perfectly logical.

In reality, these sentiments may have much more to do with a perception of the ends, the idea that some grave danger lies in leaving books unbanned or allowing certain speakers a stage. Upon this basis, the conclusion of infringing upon some civil liberty to address the issue is perfectly rational, a cost well worth paying.

Alas, many don't share the basis, and what follows, to them, is a reinforcement of the notion that the Other Side is unreasonable and immoral, that their values are different and somehow wrong. Each such assessment brings with it a greater alienation and a greater inflammation of our tensions. And with each such moment, we draw a small step closer to a dangerous escalation we should all hope to avoid.

Looking Inward

If we are to try to heal our politics as a society, it would stand to reason that we should start with the way that we perceive and handle politics as individuals. It is natural, after all, to fall into a frame of mind that inflames our thoughts, and no one of us is above the temptation of treating it as sport (and all the sense of passion and community which follows) or as religion (and all the sense of purpose and affirmation that accompanies it).

These temptations are heightened at a time when many more of us lack a proper sense of community, or a well-realized sense of purpose and deeper meaning. I, myself, am no stranger to turning toward politics for validation and a sense of fulfillment, and the amazing people I have met along my journey certainly do make me want to see them happy, and to rejoice and celebrate alongside them.

These aren't inherently bad things, but we need always to ask ourselves—does our passion around the issues and the figures of our day make it harder for us to endure criticism, to persuade those outside our ideological group, or to refine and articulate our ideas in a way that can speak and make sense to different audiences? Is our sense of self-certainty and conviction, even if compelling for those in our in-group, off-putting to those outside? Are we limiting our reach by adhering to the language and moral declarations we use to assert our political identity?

The importance we place on issues tends not to waver, and sometimes, the only way to work through it is by internalizing the idea that we serve our causes better by becoming more effective ambassadors, and we become more effective ambassadors through civil discourse. Likewise, we can attain some humility—even if we're personally quite sure on where we stand—by putting our beliefs in context, understanding our role in the broader conversation, and even by appreciating the sheer complexity of the problems we're trying to solve. Through this, we may be better able to embrace a more constructive approach, and to realize the benefits of offering an open mind.

---

1. Henry, William A. "Press: Another Rush to Judgment." TIME, nextgen, 19 Nov. 1984

2. Cooperman, Alan. "Most U.S. Parents Pass along Their Religion and Politics to Their Children." *Pew Research Center*, 10 May 2023

3. "The Psychology of Sports Fandom | Psychology Today."

5

The People Games Play

Power, Corruption, and Where the Incentives Lie

S ometimes, when I'm exhausted from thinking about polarization
and corruption and party-building, I turn to basketball—well,
mostly podcasts about it. Ironically, it's when I've turned my attention
here that I've found some of my greatest insights into the nature of
governance and into society as a whole. Precisely because it isn't so
politicized, the world of basketball makes it easier to recognize complex
power structures, distorting incentives, and the natural tendency toward
imbalance for the things they are.

Bear with me, here.

Let's look at the NBA draft, for instance. Every year, sixty of the
world's most promising basketball prospects are selected in a two-round
ordered process by the league's 30 professional franchises. To create some
sense of balance and fairness, teams with the worst records from the
prior season are given top selections by way of a weighted lottery system.
Unfortunately, the manipulable nature of having the worst record, combined with the profound impact a superstar pick can have, encourages
many teams to trade players away and rest (that is, not play) what players
they have, in search of better odds. These "tanking" teams, along with
many chronically mismanaged franchises, are often rewarded with the
best incoming talent, but the natural alternative—more balanced, or
flattened, lottery odds—would reduce things to something of a crap-

shoot, going against the intent of the record-based draft, and limiting its ability to maintain competitive fairness.

The draft, as well as all other league business, is overseen by a commissioner, tasked with both representing and balancing the interests of the thirty franchise owners. Together, they set the rules, but they're not the only power in play. There is plenty of opportunity, and plenty of incentive, for others to try to leverage their position within the multibillion-dollar industry, and team executives, players (represented by the players' association), and even agents have done just that.

Why is this important? Because these same phenomena—twisted incentives, complex and dynamic power structures—permeate so many facets of our society. To assess them analytically, beyond the politicized lens, allows us not only to better understand the critical issues at hand, but to unlock a common language we can use to discuss them. **Concerns we might have assumed only our ideological group could appreciate, from the corruptibility and inefficiency of Big Government, to the anti-competitive nature of corporations, to the harm individuals are capable of inflicting upon one another, can coexist on the same plane, each informing a constructive dialogue in which all of us can take part.**

The applications are not limited to economic issues. Whatever the topic, understanding the big-picture dynamics involved allows us to break down our assumptions of what it means to think about and discuss politics, and to embrace and engage in a better kind of discourse. But we'll start here.

Hating the Game

If we examine more broadly what economic power means in the modern age, and where it drives the behaviors of individuals and industry, we find a system that is inherently quite entropic, trending toward greater and greater imbalance. And when our elected politics are driven more toward noise and energy than actual solutions, the problems compound upon themselves. The system becomes broken.

Now, some may contend that such a system *is* working—it's simply rigged. This may well be true—I'd certainly be hard pressed to convince them otherwise—but there are a few reasons the lens of systemic failure is essential here.

First, these two theories—the system is broken, and the system is rigged—aren't mutually exclusive. It is entirely possible that some malicious intent is in place, or malicious actors in key positions of oversight and control. If the natural incentives alone are enough to perpetuate our trouble, however, then fixating on finding the evildoers behind it all would only do so much. Removing them, after all, wouldn't stop the machinations.

Second, the fixation on identifying some guilty party frequently ends up derailing the conversation altogether. You might think it's the Illuminati or some other Grand Cabal of conspirators, but if you can't convince others, then they'll simply ignore any conclusions drawn from such a basis. So, rather than limit your audience, taking a more common ground approach may be better to communicate your points.

Third, **calling the system rigged attributes a great deal of undue credit to those tasked with policymaking and oversight.** All too often, this line of thinking leads to a certain kind of defeatism, the idea that nothing can be changed because the oppressive strings are so perfectly taut in place.

As the old adage goes, "Don't hate the player, hate the game," though that's not exactly what I'm advocating, either. For one, you're well within your rights to hate the player, and it may well be that the weight of societal disapproval is a necessary piece of the incentive-fixing puzzle. What's more, hating the game, or even those tasked with managing the game, doesn't accomplish much. **The point is to understand why it is the way it is, and to do something about it.**

By following the incentives of our economic actors, we can understand the profound failure of our problem-solving apparatus and its own perverse incentives. We can realize the dangerous role our tribalism and its profiteers play in perpetuating and exacerbating the trouble. Maybe, just maybe, we can begin to make sense of a world seemingly gone so mad.

Making the Most of Things

In order to understand where our incentives lead, it's important to establish one simple truth about our behavior: **that we are all, by and large, trying to create the best possible outcomes for ourselves and our loved ones, and that we will use every resource and opportunity available to this end.**

These points of leverage may be the networks and connections we have access to. They may be the skills we have, and the career pathways those skills offer, or they may be as simple as our capital and our ability to spend and invest it toward a better present and future.

It's not only for ourselves. By and large, people want to provide for their families, to create comfort and security and opportunity for their children. It's natural, after all.

All across the animal kingdom, we find competition for limited resources. The faster predators may get ahead, as do those who utilize more stealth, or those who adapt to hunt at night. Over time, the most profitable behaviors are selected for, and it starts with individuals working to maximize their outcomes.

In our modern times, however, there is far more in play than genetics and evolution. Society and technology change rapidly, and we, in turn, scramble to adjust, to understand how to convert whatever advantages we have into more advantages and greater advantages. The result is a kind of entropy, a system where imbalance can lead to more imbalance, and the whole thing veers toward chaos if we don't somehow work to rein it in.

> ## We are all, by and large, trying to create the best possible outcomes for ourselves and our loved ones, and we will use every resource and opportunity available to that end.

Put simply, the rich will seek and find ways to get richer. Maybe it's a matter of collecting real estate, or any other high-yield investment with a prohibitive barrier to entry. Maybe it's a matter of having access to the best financial advisors, or the best education and career preparation. Maybe it's a matter of utilizing connections to garner some political favor. What's more, it's not only the one-percenters who do it—anyone with some sort of advantage should quite reasonably be looking to leverage it, whether the end being sought is continued prosperity or just making ends meet.

On the corporate side of things, let's examine the case of Amazon and its early tribulations. Starting in 1994 as an online bookseller, the company was losing money throughout its nascent years, hemorrhaging some $720 million during the DotCom Crash year of 2000.[1] By funneling further and further investment to absorb the shocks, however, the Washington-based tech giant managed to position itself as a key first-mover, with the scale and brand to leap on technological advances in the coming decades and start raking in record profits. As a tale of perseverance and long-term planning, it's downright inspiring, a case taught in most every business school for good reason. As a strategic precedent, however, it offers something of an Ur-example of how one can leverage a large quantity of resources to gain an even larger one.

This is not meant as an indictment. Again, we're all looking to make the most for ourselves, whatever economic position we're in. Year after year, we take whatever tax cut we can find, tap into any benefit program we have access to. Particularly in times of desperation, many throughout history have turned to more illicit means to find resources. If your family was depending on it, could you honestly say you wouldn't?

A friend once commented to me that, were he a CEO of some major company, he would take care of his employees, and pay them all a fair wage. It's a noble sentiment—and indeed, a great many share it—but it's not quite so simple as doing the right thing in the world of business.

What happens when you find yourself lagging behind lower-cost competitors in a cutthroat industry? What happens when shareholders aren't getting their expected dividends? However well-minded the intent, is the goodwill sustainable?

The business ecosystem can be brutally selective, and this becomes only truer as new technology emerges to shake things up. New opportunities mean new points of leverage and new ways to create competitive advantage and separation.

In the internet age, there is also far more ability to scale in industry. A brick-and-mortar shop or a restaurant might be bound by its capacity and the number of customers in the vicinity, but the same can't be said of a media company, of an app developer, or of an online content creator. The tops of each of these heaps dominate, becoming astronomically larger and more powerful than most of their competitors—let alone any new entrants—could ever hope to be.

> Wherever there is power, there is the potential for its abuse. Realizing this allows us to appreciate a wide range of different perspectives, and to open a gateway to the greater conversation.

Scale itself is an advantage that can be leveraged in a myriad of ways, and perhaps the most dramatic example comes in the form of the major banks and insurers deemed "Too Big to Fail" during the 2008 mortgage crisis. Buoyed by the thinking that their collapse would create societal chaos—a conclusion far from unfounded—they managed to withstand catastrophe with the help of government bailouts. With this status in mind, these titans have the potential to take risks with a sort of impunity smaller companies could only dream of.

In times of scarcity or great uncertainty, there is all the more reason to leverage every possible advantage, and greater risk in not doing so. Supply chains face compounding costs from each layer buffering against the unknown, and the end consumer is frequently left to foot the bill.

Embiggening the Picture

The above, in essence, is a view through the systemic lens, and it is not always in our nature to take it. Doing so when analyzing issues, however, may not be as difficult as you might imagine, and it may hold the key to being able to drive conversations and problem-solving with a wide range of audiences.

Most often, when we discuss politics, we focus on a particular incident or piece of news. These aren't small concerns, and I don't intend to make light of them, but with the right toolset, we can build a bridge from these particulars to a more fundamental and accessible conversation.

Chief among the things we need is a framework we'll be coming back to quite a bit, and this is the idea of **misuse of power**. Power takes many forms, and realizing its universality as a concept is essential to making sense of a range of different worldviews.

When it comes to problems of labor, we have, of course, the potential for corporations to abuse their power at the expense of employees (by way of worsening conditions or paying less) or the public (by way of charging more or not ensuring quality and safety). But labor unions, too, have the potential to misuse their power at the expense of individual laborers and new market entrants (by stifling competition) or the consuming public (by driving up costs). Even the individual worker or consumer has abusable power, manifesting for example through their ability to litigate frivolously or excessively against unions or businesses. Effective, comprehensive labor policy needs to take all of this into account.

When it comes to guns, there is power in the individual, through their arms-bearing liberty, that can be abused, has been abused, and needs to be accounted for in practical policymaking. There is potential also for misuse and abuse of power by the government and its enforcing agencies, or by other elements in the society—criminals, for instance—when stricter controls are in place.

It is not only government that can be wasteful and inefficient, nor only corporations that can leverage their scale at the expense of others, nor only individuals that can be reckless and short-sighted. **Wherever there is power, there is the potential for its abuse. Realizing this allows us to appreciate a wide range of different perspectives, and to open a gateway to the greater conversation.**

Incentives, corruption and corruptibility, and power dynamics, furthermore, aren't restricted to economic issues, and understanding their further application can vastly expand our analytical toolset. Whatever the issue, looking toward the big picture and utilizing frameworks like this helps us to process and communicate our thoughts and concerns, even when those we're talking to are fixated on some other piece of the puzzle.

The Convoluted Confusion of Complexity

It needs to be said, however, that being able to process and discuss an issue at hand is a far cry from being able to solve it. We're dealing with serious societal problems, after all, and they tend not to be simple ones.

Some of the reasons for their complexity are things we've already touched on. These are the myriad potential misuses of power, the difficulties of implementing, enforcing, and scaling policy, and all of the moral considerations at hand from all of the plethora of perspectives we need to consider.

When it comes to economic issues, we can also add to this list the intricacies of global supply chains and the potential for disruption through various acts of God or man. Of course, we have a world of incentives to consider, including those of actors outside our country who may be influenced by policies in which we have no say.

But wait, there's more! An entire branch of economics is dedicated to just how deep these things can get. It's most commonly called Complexity Economics, and it talks all about complex adaptive systems—alternatively, second-order complex systems—wherein macro-level economic phenomena emerge by way of heterogenous agents adapting behaviors to the changing realities of an economic system which lies in constant flux because of the heterogenous agents adapting behaviors to its changing realities.

If all of that seems complicated, good! The point is not to immediately understand everything in play, but to appreciate how hard it would be to do so. Even with the best tools and the most thorough possible process, finding effective solutions is going to be difficult. **But if we fail**

to communicate or analyze our problems constructively, and if we have leadership and governance which reflects that failure, then solving those problems becomes nigh impossible.

More Patterns of Divergence

As new exploits and optimal strategies make themselves known within any economic system or power structure, the rules—if the system is well managed—should be adjusted to ensure fairness, lest the other players revolt (figuratively, for the most part). This, after all, is why we have antitrust laws, why we have restrictions against insider trading, why we have unions and labor laws, and so forth.

When we aren't seeing new corrections, however, and when the entropic corruption is allowed to grow further and further, it behooves us to take a look at those tasked with managing these systems, so to speak, why they aren't being effective in doing so, and what incentives of their own might have something to do with it.

In the first portion of this book, I talked about how our governance becomes less and less effective as people fall into more polarization, alienation, and tribal emotion. The trouble, however, goes beyond this, because, all the while, our problems aren't just persisting—they're getting worse. There are constantly new exploits being found, new layers to the supply chains, new sources of chaos and uncertainty.

A sense of alarm or panic does us no good, but a sense of urgency is absolutely warranted. It is not only that the problems at hand are themselves critical to the quality of our lives, to our rights and liberties, and to our very existence. It is also that the longer we go in our current state, the harder solving these problems—if we can break out of our polarized paralysis—is going to become.

The good news is, even if we appreciate the difficulty inherent in finding functional solutions, we can still contribute positively to understanding the challenges we face and driving a more constructive process toward overcoming them. It is *because* of all the complexity involved, in fact, that our unique voices and perspectives are so needed.

We may not individually have all the answers or the full scope of the big picture, but we each hold our part of it. If we can share that part with others looking from differing perspectives, then this gives us the best chance to inform real answers and determine effective solutions. And if we can bring this mindset to others and demonstrate its success, then we might even be able to fix our problem-solving apparatus before it's too late.

---

1. Agustin, Francis. ""We Are Famously Unprofitable": A 36-Year-Old Jeff Bezos on Amazon." Bbc.com, BBC, July 2024

6

Seeking the Common Goal
First Steps to Collaborative Discourse

Why do we approach politics the way we do? Why do we argue so passionately, so loudly, so violently at times? Why do we argue at all?

There are many answers to the above, of course, from the weight and importance we attribute to the issues themselves, to the way we marry our egos to what we stand for and how we stand for it. But there is also the reality that we often act as we do because it's the way we know how, and we lose sight at times that there may be other ways.

This is not advocating for civil discourse on some grand moral ground. You may well be justified in your passion, in your anger, in the fire with which you declare your beliefs. But being fiery is a fine tool to energize, and a terrible one to convince those who disagree. **Conflict mentality undermines our ability to be the best communicators we can be, and ultimately to bring about the positive change that we should want to see.**

In the worlds of business and science, it is well understood that you achieve the best results by welcoming different perspectives and by offering and embracing constructive feedback. As wild as it may seem, approaching politics collaboratively leads to more productive, more positive conversations. You'll learn more, communicate more points more effectively, and feel better at the end of the day.

One of the best summations of a collaborative mindset comes from the world of relationship counseling, and boils down to this: **when you're in a disagreement, remember that it isn't really you against your partner. It's both of you against the problem.**

It may feel weird at first to apply that kind of thinking here. You'll get used to it.

We're All in This Together (No, Really)

Now that we've established it'd be fantastic if we could work together, it's worth facing the question—why should we? What are we working together *toward*? What if we don't agree on the destination?

For many, this is where the prospects for any sort of mutual collaboration fall apart, because, as they assume, the sides of our discourse have entirely opposite goals. And yet, the mainstreams of both Left and Right would contradict this.

The Right, for decades, has insisted that lower taxes and industry-friendly policy help everyone, and that the wealth will spread. The Left says aid to the lower classes, including access to educational resources, empowers our industry and helps us compete on the world stage. The Right says we have better safety with legal access to guns. The Left says we have better public health with legal access to various drugs. The list goes on, and in practically every one of these cases, the advocating side would say their solution is a no-brainer, and that no real sacrifices are required.

Yes, some more fringe voices outwardly wish ill to the Other Side, but by and large, the idea of public policy as a zero-sum game with constant tradeoffs is overstated. We may disagree fundamentally on how to reach them, but in the end we want many of the same things.

> Conflict mentality undermines our ability to be the best communicators we can be, and ultimately to bring about the positive change that we should want to see.

We all gain from children having the opportunity to realize their potential. Yes, we may disagree on where the critical barriers are, or how to lower them. We may disagree, for instance, whether an emphasis on inclusivity helps more or less than victim mentality inhibits, or if early exposure to certain ideas and content is healthy. But we want what we see ultimately as best for the kids, because we want them to become the best possible leaders and innovators and citizens of tomorrow.

Likewise, we all gain when our young people develop strong moral character, when they support their communities and don't go out harming others for personal gain. Yes, even if we disagree on what the most essential values are, or how to instill them.

We all gain from creating economic opportunity, that inspires people to produce and allows them to dream. Of course, we argue about how best to create it, and, as we've well established, the economy is a complicated and ever-evolving beast.

And we all gain from having a people who feel empowered and heard, though we struggle, in these divided days, to create that feeling for anyone outside the current ruling tribe, or for anyone whose own views should deviate.

All of these are complex problems, but they are problems we can work to solve *together*. Realizing this is an essential first step not only to understanding the importance of dialogue, but to making it work.

Wearing the Right Hat

The second step, then, is understanding how we as individuals can take part in the important conversations—and sometimes the difficult conversations—that we need to have. This shouldn't require changing your views, and it doesn't. It may help, however, to consider the manner in which you frame and present your ideas.

The way we've become accustomed to discussing opinions isn't meant to sway or change minds; it's meant to energize or vent. Grand statements of our principles—"housing is a human right," "taxation is theft," and so forth—don't lend themselves to debate or conversation. What they are good at is getting people to nod and pump their fists in agreement—if they're predisposed to agree anyway.

In essence, what we're doing by focusing on these declaratives is playing the role of philosophers, arguing in perpetuity about what is Good and True and Worthy, and sometimes why. Philosophers write their books about how the world ought to be, occasionally reference and try to refute one another, and cater, for the most part, to their individual audiences. **In the end, they don't have to work together, but we as a society do.**

Instead, you can play the role of legislator, a member of a problem-solving team, working to understand what it is you want to do with your principles and how they affect the way you view policy. Where do you see the potential for societal good in the ideas you would support, or for societal error or harm in the alternatives? What are the key points you would look to advocate for, or the factors you would want to ensure are well considered?

Most importantly, you should be ready to make your case to someone who might not hold all of your same values, and who might not be convinced to do so. How might a more liberal housing policy improve neighborhood safety and bolster local businesses? How might government-run programming lead to waste, inefficiency, or a lack of effective oversight in particular areas?

It may be an odd sensation at first when you let go of your hard-set declarations, when you appreciate when they might not be shared. Good—that's the start of a healthy conversation. Don't be afraid to ask questions you may not know the answers to, or to consider scenarios and perspectives you might not have fully fleshed out.

Building the bridge, between the ideas that we hold on one side, and a healthy, productive discourse on the other, isn't easy. For us or any other democratic society, however, our success is tied inextricably to whether we can make the most of our ability to work together and integrate different perspectives. This ability, after all, is part of what makes us human.

A Brief Aside on Our Fundamental Nature

Our capacity to collaborate—thinking together, working together, complementing one another—is not only the reason that we have democracy. This ability is one of the integral elements that makes society possible.

Humans are social animals, and our social structures function largely because of our differences. Some of us want to be hunters, some gatherers. Some are adept at science, some are gifted in and drawn to the arts, and some derive the greatest joy from teaching. The supply of each role doesn't always perfectly match the demand, but ultimately these are the complementary elements that make our civilization what it is—or at least, the positive aspects thereof.

Why should politics be any different? At the core of the liberal mindset is the constant desire to question, to challenge, and to change our structures and laws in service of a better and more just future. It an essential motivating force, particularly as our world changes and our sensibilities shift, but it is buoyed by having the presence of conservative thought to remind us why our structures sometimes need to be the way they are, and what harm we might risk by upending them. The same is true in reverse—a conservative mindset is great for appreciating what works and what is best to maintain, but it is, in fact, helped tremendously by welcoming a reformist perspective on what may not be working so well, and what alternatives may be available.

Likewise, it is the presence of fiery and passionate thought that spurs us to action and alerts us first to injustice. But it is moderate sentiment that tempers our rush and soothes potential volatility. Keeping these in balance isn't easy, but it's important to appreciate what each provides.

This diversity in ways of thinking is an incredible asset if we can make use of it. The broader the range that we can incorporate into healthy conversation—assuming we can foster healthy conversation—the more we can learn and consider, and the stronger the solutions we produce will be.

Waging War Against Conflict Mentality

We can accomplish incredible things by working together, thinking together, and learning from others who view the world differently. This is the core of any kind of constructive dialogue, and the key to preparing ourselves for it—the thing that all of this reflection and introspection has been building up to—lies in conquering our own conflict mindset.

The mentality of constant conflict is more dangerous in our modern age than it has ever been before. There are far more traps leading into it, far more temptation to shelter inside our bubbles and surround ourselves with tribal fervor. All the while, more and more of our media, corporations, and politicians are capitalizing on our divisions—not because they're evil, necessarily, but because those divisions are easy to take advantage of, and it would be foolish from a business sense not to try and profit.

In reality, those of different political persuasions do not have to be your enemy, and you gain nothing by viewing them as such. They are, by and large, trying to preach and follow their values, drawn as so many of us are to the sense of community and the sense of purpose that politics can provide. You may be able yet to reach to people, to work with them, and to learn from them, if you know how.

The same holds even for those who take advantage of our divisions or any other faults or weaknesses in our structures and institutions. By and large, they are leveraging what resources and advantages they have to make the most for themselves and those around them, as most any of us would. Should their exploits be outlawed and penalized? Quite possibly, as that's one of the ways that our systems can be improved. **But we are not going to solve our systemic problems simply by labeling their profiteers as our enemies.**

At our core, we understand that we have the ability to collaborate, to challenge each other and grow from each other. This is why we have innovations and inventions. This is why we have achieved so much of what we have achieved. It is a power that we all have, a power we can apply to solving any societal issue before us.

Bringing a common-goal orientation into the political realm takes work. It demands a deliberate mindset to start the process, and some important tools and frameworks to be able to fully incorporate our perspectives into productive dialogue—of course, we'll be getting to those.

It is not an easy battle, but we can make tremendous strides by simply understanding what the battle is, **realizing that we need to try to overcome not each other, but our conflict-mad notions of what politics is and how we can engage with it.**

Now, let's go win that battle—together.

Intermission

The Insatiable Lust for Power that Drives Us All

A little while back, I mentioned that we're all trying to do the best for ourselves and those close to us, and that this essential driving force is one of the things we have in common. But there's more to this.

We also want to have a sense of control over the road ahead, over our futures and our fates. It is one of the defining aspects of the human condition, and an essential lens through which to view both our political moment and how we can escape it.

People want stability when it comes to what they have, and mobility when it comes to what they can achieve if they do their best. They want to be able to utilize their resources to have influence and impact, to make the world more like they want to see it, whether they stand as billionaires looking to exert influence or commonfolk who just want their voices heard.

When leaders, elected to inspire confidence and hope and a positive sense of societal direction, fail repeatedly over the course of decades, the people are going to look elsewhere for empowerment. They will reject what they view as broken institutions, and they will seek to empower themselves. The result is chaos and confusion, discord and disunity, and occasionally disaster.

What makes our current cycles of division most volatile is the sense of constant despair and futility they create. We feel helpless to do anything but watch as things get worse and worse. Within this darkness, however, may lie our greatest opportunity to do something about it.

Because upstream of a broken system of governance is a people struggling to communicate with one another. It is a problem that goes well beyond politics, and into the alienation and hopelessness that plague all too many. These are critical issues that create a colossal demand for solutions, even among those unconcerned with depolarization or the duopoly or any other political balderdash.

I say all this not as an outside observer, but as someone who has fought for years—personally as well as professionally—against this sense of hopelessness, as someone frustrated and exhausted by the difficulty of breaking through the noise when the noise is bringing and amplifying so much destruction.

It is because of this experience that I set out to write this book, because I understand the tremendous need for a sense of empowerment and control when it comes to our society's future. If we are able to speak to this need, and if we are able to offer something of worth to address it, then this may be our greatest opportunity to move the needle and drive toward something better.

As I said at the outset, this is not a plea for civility for the sake of civility. **This is a guide to help you, no matter where you stand on any spectrum, to get your ideas across, to feel heard and to make others feel heard, and, if you should so choose, to be the change we need in our democracy.**

Together, I believe truly that we can build common ground, a means by which we can better communicate, better work together, and better function as a society. Where we go from there, and what we plant upon that ground, is entirely up to you.

PART III

---◆---

Leveling the Field

YOUR GOAL: Be Curious

Well, here we are—the part where I give you a bunch of conversational tips and tricks so you can talk to your great-uncle without losing your mind. I hope you're as excited as I am.

There's much more to it, of course, and it's worth acknowledging again here that I'm not the first to offer such a thing, and giving some brief shouts-out to the authors and organizers in whose footsteps I follow.

Justin Lee is, as he puts it, an LGBTQ Christian activist, who understandably has some experience navigating between groups who might tend to disagree. His 2018 book, *Talking Across the Divide,* explores the barriers standing against meaningful dialogue—our egos, our loyalties, our love of comfort, and our possible misinformation, among other things—and how we can overcome them. It's a great read, and if you enjoy this one, I do recommend checking it out.

Two years after Lee's book came out, Tania Israel released *Beyond Your Bubble: How to Connect Across the Political Divide.* Dr. Israel is a trained psychologist (and Professor of Counseling Psychology at UC Santa Barbara, as of this writing), and her expertise shines through in the example-rich exploration of positive political dialogue. Again, definitely worth checking out if you're interested.

Beyond the dedicated books and other media, there are also plenty of dialogue-focused non-profits and community organizations with their own methodology around how people with different views can have civil conversations. Though they generally require all parties to opt in—which can be limiting—they tend to garner positive responses for those who do take part, and I have no interest in speaking ill of them.

The main differences in this text from any of the above lay in the reasons I give to seek things out, the ways I try to make ideas more accessible and appealing to different persuasions, and the connections I explore between the need for a shift in conversational mindset shift to upstream political and cultural drivers, as well as downstream to political and cultural impacts. All of which is to say, some of the core ideas on how to have these more positive conversations are similar to those in other guides, primarily because a lot of these ideas are well-known.

In truth, there is no "killer app" when it comes to being able to hold a conversation with someone you disagree with, to present your viewpoints in a way they can better understand, or to make sense of why they believe what they believe. What matters far more than the specific words you choose, more than the tone of your voice, more than the number of seconds you speak before asking someone their thoughts, is the mindset you bring in. **Above all, if you want to enjoy positive transformation through political dialogue, the best thing you can do is be curious.**

Viewing every political encounter as a fight begets a sense of constant conflict, and it will feel stressful and awful. Viewing the same encounters as learning opportunities, however, wherein you get to better understand different worldviews and perspectives and ideas, allows you to walk away from each with a feeling of accomplishment and growth.

Remember, it's not just for you. Your partners in conversation can open their minds and hearts if they see you embracing a more positive approach. If you are, in fact, right, and they are, in fact, wrong, then it's going to help them to be able to see that light. And if you can take your newfound ability to communicate and articulate and drive it toward positive societal change through your ideas, then we all stand to gain.

The goal here (other than to be curious) is to understand that the real winning to be found through political dialogue is through positive, personal transformation. You can learn about yourself and your partners in conversation, and you can learn how to build bridges across any divide you face.

What is being leveled by these tools is not a playing field—first, because we don't mix metaphors here, and, second, because there is no game to worry about playing. Rather, this is the field of our common ground, where we might plant seeds not only of healthy conversation but fruitful conversation, the sort of dialogue that can lead us to both personal growth and societal breakthroughs.

7

Transformative Growth with Confucius

And Jesus, Too

S ome 2,500 years ago, the philosopher Confucius was approached by
his disciple, Zi Gong. Zi, apparently not in any mood to meander,
asked the sage if any single word can guide a person throughout life.

> *"How about 'shu' [reciprocity],"* replies the master, *"never
> impose on others what you would not choose for yourself?"*[1]

With this exchange from the *Analects*, Confucius establishes one of
the most famous examples of the Golden Rule, or what some philosophers term the principle or ethic of reciprocity. It may be presented
either in the negative, as above, or in the positive—to do unto others as
you would wish done to yourself—and has appeared in some form in
most every major religion, from the teachings of Jesus to the texts of the
Yoruba. It's also made its way into plenty of nonreligious ethical texts, as
well.

The power of the Golden Rule lies in this universality, and in the fact
that it has been ingrained so deeply in our common psyche. Intrinsically,
people know to reciprocate, to respond to hostility with hostility, and to
kindness more often in kind (though not always, and it's important not
to get taken advantage of).

The Rule is essential to how we build friendships, how we build
relationships, and how we build trust. In the realm of discourse, it's a

key to how we can become more persuasive and effective advocates of what we believe, but to utilize it fully requires taking an important, and sometimes difficult, first step.

The Art of Reciprocity

When we talk about striving to be better at discussing politics, the goal for many of us—and it's okay to admit it—is to convince others to come to our side of an argument. We want to be more persuasive in the ideas we present. We want the people with whom we're talking to consider what it is we have to say, to open their minds, and, ideally, to change them.

Here's the secret: **if you want someone to change their mind, it helps to be willing to change your own.**

That's really it. Come in with an open mind and a genuine curiosity, and people will be much more likely to engage in an open and curious discussion—the kind where minds, every so often, do change.

The task may seem daunting at first, and it's one some may view with the apprehension that an open mind is some sign of weakness to be taken advantage of. One of the longstanding arguments against the Golden Rule, after all, is that unconditional generosity is all too easy to exploit. Factor in the distrust many of us carry when engaging with those with whom we disagree, and this wariness becomes all the more understandable.

It is possible, however, to offer an open mind and still take things with a grain of salt. You can still be thorough in taking whatever you're presented with under consideration, checking the facts and their sources and their counterarguments, and doing your proper research. If this approach, of a willingness to carefully consider, is enough to want in kind, then it's no risk to be the first to put it forward.

It is worth remembering that being willing to change your mind doesn't obligate you to change your mind. In the same way a hardened and unwavering approach invokes defensiveness and hostility, however, showing a genuine curiosity can inspire people you might not expect to ever let their guard down to open up and, well, reciprocate.

It's an invaluable mindset shift, and the key to embracing it lies in accepting the idea that you can learn something from hearing a different perspective. And if you don't agree, well, then I would invite you, politely, to reconsider.

Be Humble...

To accept that there is more to learn from different perspectives is one of the most essential steps in moving from having miserable, repetitive shouting matches, to being able to hold conversations that are fulfilling and even transformational—a concept we'll get to in a bit. Central to this approach is accepting that you, and by extension your "team"—if you identify with one—don't own all the answers. This applies whether you identify as being Left, Right, Center, or anywhere else along the great political continuum.

This is not to say your worldview is wrong. Rather, the critical thing to accept is that you may benefit from hearing different perspectives.

Conversely, if you can acknowledge a few cases of potential excess or error in tuning those other perspectives out, that should be reason enough to maintain an open mind.

> # If you really want someone to change their mind, it helps to be willing to change your own.

If you identify with the political left, then you may need only to consider those cases where nationalization of services creates costly inefficiency, or rapid reforms make for unsustainable policy. These points may seem obvious at times, and their purpose is not to make you abandon your post—only to help internalize that there may be value in hearing those other voices.

Likewise, if you find yourself on the right, it may help to think of the potential for error or abuse in putting too much power in industry, the private sector, or even the individual. It may help to consider any past institutions which became ill-suited to modern situations, or that eventually required reform. It may help to think of any exceptions to the statements or ideas you generally support, any case where a policy that sounded promising didn't quite turn out as you'd hoped.

All the above applies to the center, too. "Meeting in the middle" does not lend itself automatically to effective policy. Neither does incremental change, nor does any other third-way methodology. Any case of compromise for the sake of compromise leading to twisted or strange incentives—for instance, private sector subsidization contributing to price inflation on health care, education, or housing—can help reinforce this. As with any standard partisan, rejecting the sense of entitlement to being the Bearer of Truth allows us to better adopt the intellectual humility a healthy discourse demands.

You may feel that you already take some excesses and exceptions into account, and that yours is a more tuned and reasoned version of whatever philosophy you espouse. This very well may be, but the notion that there is nothing to be gained from hearing disagreement can lead down a dangerous road.

Within the space of non-partisan political activism—a space I have long worked in—a number of people have claimed to offer an unobjective and unbiased truth. Usually, this is provided through some sort of reporting medium, and typically it is offered in service of none other than common ground, in the sense of what we can all agree on and unite around. Unfortunately, it tends not to work out this way.

At best, these efforts tend to be somewhat naïve, underestimating the bias inherent in the language we use, the framing of data and statistics, and what we choose to talk about in the first place. At worst, they exemplify a kind of arrogance, the notion of a perfectly informed and objective guiding beacon of truth that needs no further correction. In striving toward objectivity, they abandon humility, putting forward the implication that whatever facts and points they present are ineligible for argument.

Nobody is perfect. No one is the single arbiter of truth, and no one needs to be. We are all subject to the biases of our limited perspectives and experiences and the ideas we've been exposed to. Each of us, however, can play a role in the greater conversation, and in this conversation there is always more to learn.

So, embrace it. Be curious. Ask questions—not only the stances of others, but how they reach these stances, and why what resonates with them so resonates.

As you embrace this learning process, your partners in conversation will notice, will feel heard, and will return the favor more than you might expect.

... But Confident

To accept you have more to learn and consider is not to say you have nothing yourself to offer. For every one of my readers, I know this is not the case, that each one of you has the opportunity to better our society through your insights and your perspective. Yes, you have more to learn—but you already have something to bring to the table.

This something is your voice, after all, your expression. You are a member of our democratic society with a unique experience and outlook to contribute, and this should absolutely be something to be proud of.

It helps in discourse to acknowledge our biases and the limitations in our perspective, but even with this self-awareness, you can be clear and confident in presenting your thoughts. Share why you think certain things resonate with you, how your beliefs have evolved and developed over time, how various influences have helped mold your political identity. Though you understand that your ideas are simply your ideas, there should be no shame in wearing them with conviction.

And if your ideas aren't fully formed, that's okay too. You can be honest with what you've found so far, and with what causes you confusion and uncertainty. There is nothing wrong with being unsure, and such transparency can go a long way in fostering healthy conversation and even building deeper trust in more personal settings.

Straw Men Tell Tall Tales

Your story matters, from the foundations of your beliefs to the experiences and perceptions which shape your ideas today. It is not only something that you *deserve* to be able to share—I try not to think about things in those terms—but something that can deeply benefit those with whom you engage in dialogue. As such, one of the worst things you can do to the prospects of a constructive conversation is to deny your partner the chance to share their own.

Doing so, in essence, is *strawmanning*—building up a caricature of your opponent's argument to make it easier to refute and dismiss. It amounts to handwaving away whatever the other person has to say, often reducing it to its most unflattering interpretation. How would you expect someone to respond to this? How would you?

You may well feel you've heard certain points and perspectives before. You can say so honestly, presenting your understanding of what a particular counterargument is, and what it is that doesn't resonate or make sense to you. There is a dramatic difference, however, between putting this information forward with a genuine curiosity (and genuinely inviting a response), and indicating that someone else's beliefs aren't worth listening to.

The operative concept remains reciprocity. If we show dismissal and disdain, we can expect to be met with dismissal and disdain. Instead, we can choose to show open minds in hopes that our partners in conversation will do the same, and we can share our thoughts and views to encourage others to return with their own. Through these steps, we can foster the kind of conversation and the kind of discourse that we ourselves would want to take part in—discourse which is fulfilling, enlightening, and enjoyable.

Choose Your Words Wisely

It's worth starting to zoom in here, to observe how a broader mind-set shift can manifest in the more precise aspects of conversation. Each decision we make—and indeed, each word—can help make the difference between a draining and destructive spat, and a fulfilling and productive dialogue.

If you find yourself baffled by what your partner in conversation is claiming about some issue, avoid phrases like "that's stupid" or "you can't possibly believe such things." Make it clear that your disagreement is your own, personal disagreement, and offer something less hostile. Maybe something along the lines of "I see it differently," followed by your best understanding of why.

Alternatively, if your partners in conversation seem not to be resonating with what you have to offer, there's no need for "you just don't get it" or similar put-downs. Dig into why, and try to find the nature of the disconnect. This curiosity will be reciprocated more often than you may expect.

And if you should find that you simply have a different understanding of the facts at hand, don't be so quick to agree to disagree. It is possible to pivot from a discussion of facts to a discussion of underlying principles and concerns, to navigate around this wall. You can also remind your conversation partner that their insistence upon certain facts may be limiting their ability to reach differing audiences, and use this to motivate a broader and more thoughtful discussion about policy and its potential for error. We'll be exploring both of these techniques in the coming chapters.

Above all, the thought and care you put into your words offer a signal that the dialogue matters to you. That learning from your partner in conversation matters to you. That maintaining and strengthening your relationship matters to you. And yes, all of that can be reciprocated, too.

Nobody is perfect. No one is the single arbiter of truth, and no one needs to be. But each of us plays a role in the greater conversation, and in this conversation there is always more to learn.

Now, your partner may be apprehensive at first if they're not used to a more collaborative tone and tenor of discourse. To this, you can explain, simply and honestly, why you've taken the route.

They may also be apprehensive if they're not used to hearing the tone from *you*, if it's a stark deviation from how you usually go about debating. If you're a firebrand type giving a collaborative approach a chance, then, first of all, thank you! But again, honesty is the best policy here, and all you need to do is explain why you decided to give it a try—and maybe, why they should, too.

Embrace Transformation

The notion of transformational leadership comes from yet another field more accustomed to collaborative thinking than the political—this time, the world of business. It's a style defined by adaptability, by making employees feel heard and listened to, and by dynamic strategizing toward a shared goal.

Likewise, so-called transformational or transformative approaches have also emerged in fields from consulting to conflict resolution. The common thread is a willingness and ability to change through consistent and thoughtful communication, and all of this can very much apply, and be put to tremendous use, in the world of politics as well.

By approaching discourse with curious minds and collaborative mindsets, we allow ourselves to shift focus from "winning" the argument, to growing from the conversation. This change makes for a far less stressful experience, and a far higher success rate.

The "transformation" aspect of things doesn't mean your opinions have to constantly change—that's not going to happen. Rather, the growth may come through having your perspectives better informed and arguments better tested, through learning more about what drives those with whom you might not agree, or even through fostering greater empathy and understanding with someone you may have had challenges communicating with in the past. Whatever the case, it is this sense of personal growth, and not any imaginary score, that tells us in no uncertain terms that we have succeeded.

This process helps us to find our own voice and our own ideas—ideas that are more captivating and compelling, more able to bring good as they make their way to others. It allows us to better inspire others and empower them to speak their own voices. It can create a mutual sense of positivity and fulfillment that is enviable, that those more used to combative and stressful forms of dialogue will want to learn and emulate.

This is the goal. And with this goal in mind, it's time to get down to brass tax—and the other pressing issues of the day—and understand what putting this approach into practice looks like, and what it takes to make it happen.

---

1. Confucius. *The Analects*. Tr. David Hinton Counterpoint LLC, 1998.

8

Finding the Common Language
Techniques for Tackling Tough Topics Together

Having a positive and curious mindset is a huge step toward gaining more from your dialogue with others. I could even go so far as to say that it's all you need in order to have amazing and productive conversations on any topic. This, however, would be a lie, and I don't want to lie to you. I owe you better than that.

I think back to a debate I attended some years ago, run by a civil-discourse-minded nonprofit. The question posed for discussion was, "Is America the greatest country on Earth?" What followed, guided by heavy moderation and strict rules on decorum and procedure, was a mostly well-mannered evening of spirited discussion. It was also, in many ways, a pointless exercise.

The first problem was the question itself, a moral declaration which lends itself poorly to analytical thinking or any sort of problem-solving mindset—**because there's no problem to solve.** On top of that, virtually all of the arguments made were coded in heavy partisan language and specific to personal anecdotes and perceptions. They were ships passing each other in the night, while I looked on from a lonely perch at the lighthouse.

More than once, I've seen debates like these between opposing partisans with the best of mindsets and intentions, but without all the tools necessary to navigate through their differences. The result tends to be conversations that start friendly but lead to a kind of nowhere, ending either in mutual, amicable confusion at how the other can think the way they do, or a breakdown to familiar frustrations.

One of the problems, as it so often is, is how accustomed we've become to the rhythm of politics inside of our bubbles. The words we use, the emotions, and the values we appeal to, speak to what affirms and energizes us. These framings aren't well suited to attract outside audiences, because that's not what they were built for.

For many of us, moreover, it has become rarer these days to encounter a strongly opposing viewpoint in real life, both because of our tendencies to hang around like-minded people, and because more and more of the interaction we do have is virtual. On top of this, many of the conversations we might be having never happen, because most of us shy from political discussion (and if you're among them, I'll remind you that his book is for you, too).

And so, what opportunities we do find, to bridge divides and better understand the Other Side, come often in the form of heated relatives, or friends and acquaintances particularly riled up about some issue or another. In these cases, our natural response—if not to try to avoid the conversation—is to assert and declare, to speak our truth. Our truth, unfortunately, can be difficult for an outside audience to understand.

A few chapters back, I talked about the importance of understanding issues through an analytical lens, appreciating their complexity as we make sense of various perspectives. **Now, it's time to take those ideas and apply them to the realm of conversation, to understand what we need to do to frame our own perceptions into language that is more conducive to healthy conversation, more accessible outside our bubbles, and more persuasive to our partners in conversation.**

Move Beyond the Moral Imperative

Go to most any rally, protest, or demonstration, and you'll hear some sort of emphatic chant. You'll hear riveting speeches about rights under attack, principles being violated, and the action needed to stop some injustice being perpetrated. To the crowds they play to, these points often earn boisterous applause, but they exemplify one of the great limitations of how we approach politics.

These types of calls to action are what we term *moral imperatives*—appeals to a particular value or set of values in the name of a political conclusion. To those who share the moral basis, it can be an excellent tool for powerful and moving rhetoric. Not everyone, however, share the moral basis.

Many of these underlying moral axioms and assertions—be they the sanctity of the Second Amendment, a woman's right to choose, the ill intent of the Deep State, or anything else—are far from universally held. If we want someone outside our ideological group to agree with our imperative, we often find ourselves having to try to convince them of its bases—and this is no easy task.

It can be deeply frustrating when others don't share our values. It *is* frustrating and dismaying for many that the principles they hold dear aren't more commonly held. This, however, is the reality of our time, and it leaves us often at an impasse if we don't know how—or don't try—to work around it.

Moral foundations are inflexible—even the most open-minded among us would seldom consider changing our values, especially in the course of a conversation. And if you're expecting others to without being willing to bend at all yourself, well, that isn't very fair, now, is it?

What we cannot do to break this kind of impasse is pretend that the moral underpinnings of our beliefs don't exist—they do, and they matter to us. We can, however, realize that there is more to support the things we believe in than our personal sense of justice, and that it is possible to be effective advocates even when our audience doesn't share our virtues.

The reality is that we think and view the world differently, and this in itself is not going to change any time soon. Even when the perceptions seem to be far apart, however, they can still be understood through a common language and a common framework—if we have the tools to do so.

Ask the Important Questions

Beyond the problem of the moral imperative, one of the most common pitfalls found in discourse is a fixation on particulars. Whenever a controversy arises, we argue and obsess over the sordid details and the individuals to blame. In an age where we get different news and different facts, any hope for finding understanding can seem to evaporate here.

To be clear, these discussions are valuable. The facts do matter, and a clearer understanding of a given case—be it a shooting, a riot, an economic event, or so on—can inform our understanding of the issues as a whole. But because these are arguments about facts, there is an inflexibility to how we approach them. We might be able to open someone to the possibility of a different version of events (rare), and we might be able to make them understand why we have ours (possible), but ultimately, this is a sort of conversation that is seldom satisfying.

The trouble is that we care so deeply about these particulars because we often understand the bigger implication—a case of police brutality shows that we're not able to uphold justice to those in power, a heinous crime by an illegal immigrant shows that we need stricter oversight, and so forth. Of course, those outside our ideological group, who don't share our broader sentiment, won't understand our outrage, and we may not be able to appreciate theirs.

Rather than leave this bigger picture implicit, or insist that it should be obvious (it isn't), what we can do instead is pivot explicitly to a conversation about the issue and the systems at hand. **We can do this by asking three crucial questions—what would you suggest, would it work, and what could go wrong?**

Collectively, these questions allow us to transition from what would be an ultimately futile partisan clash, to a line of discussion that is thought-provoking, positive, and far less likely to get derailed by differences in news source or discrepancies about particular facts.

Let's take a closer look:

What would you suggest?—the tone you strike in presenting this is essential. If you come off as sarcastic, one might read the question as implying that the solution you expect them to suggest is impossible. Especially wary audiences may suspect a trap or a-ha moment, so reassurance may be required that you're acting in good faith.

The point, of course, is to work toward a discussion of policy pros and cons, and away from a battle of philosophy against philosophy. And you can absolutely say this (it doesn't have to be word-for-word, and it may help to use your own voice) if asked—if your motives are genuine, there's no benefit in hiding them.

As important as the question itself is its follow-up. The more of an open mind that you can present in hearing what your partner in conversation suggests, the more likely they are to pay you back in kind when you talk about your own ideas.

You don't necessarily have to wait your turn, either. Be ready to offer your own inclinations, and to qualify them as inclinations *(phrases like "I've always gravitated toward..."* can be helpful framings*).* Talk about what resonates with you and why, to help guide the discussion down the road to healthy analysis.

Take your time with this. Let the temperature cool and give the conversation room to flow. Then, once the tone has been established, you can move on to the next stage, and the second key question:

Would it work?—tone, again, is crucial, as you don't want this to come across as a rhetorical trap. The truth is that you probably don't know for sure, and this should act as a reminder to approach with intellectual humility and an open mind.

To clarify, this question is not about reducing things to some objective utilitarian viewpoint, nor to any single quantifiable metric. It will not boil an issue down to simple solvable calculation, nor should it. Rather, what "working" means in this context for a policy is that *it achieves its stated goals.*

It's here that you can start to bring in data and historical examples into the discussion. Remember that there will most always be plenty to cite on both sides of a given argument, and try not to make it a competition of who offers more statistics. The purpose of this question and this exercise is to understand how best to achieve a given goal through the means of policy, and this is a journey best undertaken *together*.

If signs point to something not working, try not to be dismissive. The lesson should never be to give up on a particular objective, but instead to understand that noble ideas don't automatically translate into effective policy, and that properly making the translation demands critical eyes, constructive discourse, and a range of informing perspectives.

If you can figure out something that seems to work, then you can weigh it against well-scrutinized alternatives that prioritize other ends. Then, and only then, can you have a fully informed discussion on the tradeoffs involved and the decisions that need to be made. And yes, even that discussion can be collaborative.

This is the goal, in essence. And as you navigate your way through the conversation toward this goal, you will find yourself in the workshopping phase of things, facing the third of our crucial questions:

What could go wrong?—this, in essence, is the same common thread that ties many of our core concerns together, from misuses of power, to potential inefficiencies, to our systems' susceptibility to corruption. Each of these helps to identify potential points of failure, and collectively they give us a diverse toolset to analyze possible solutions. We can bring in our knowledge and our ideas, as well as our deeply held values, to help inform the conversation.

There are so many angles to explore. In the case of organized labor, for instance, we can examine the potential for harm in unchecked super-corporations to workers and consumers. But we can also examine the potential excesses of strong unions, and their ability to undermine the individual laborer, the consumer (from a price standpoint), or the health of the industry. We can even examine cases where the individual workers might hold too much leverage, to a point that undermines unions or somehow damages industry.

By recognizing the potential for error wherever power is placed, we can create a dynamic analysis that utilizes a diversity of perspectives. Everything adds to and informs the problem-solving process. Fundamental concerns from different parts of the political world—around government getting too much power, industry getting too much power, and even individuals having unchecked power—can exist on the same plane, all working toward the same goal of developing effective solutions.

> Three crucial questions—what would you suggest, would it work, and what could go wrong?—can help build the bridge between a frustrating argument and a fulfilling analytical exploration.

In the end, any possible policy will have some potential for error. Likelihoods and severities should be weighed. Potential tradeoffs come into view. Data can be brought in to better inform and continue the conversation. No answer will be perfect, but at the end of this exercise, you should be able to walk away with quite a bit learned, and a lot to make you think.

The goal of this, as well as with the other above questions, is to establish a functional framework to approach complex topics in a productive healthy, fulfilling manner. This framework, in turn, allows us to incorporate new considerations and new information to carry the conversation on.

Questions like these also help build an important bridge between having grand ideas about important things and being able to bring those ideas into a healthy discussion. They allow us to feel heard, and to make others feel heard, in a way modern politics rarely does. Landing here not only empowers us but allows us to heal, by affirming the power of a more collaborative discourse.

Mind the Details

Part of extending and expanding healthy policy analysis is getting into the nitty gritty. We should all be rooting for good policy that works, and so we owe it to each other to scrutinize the details.

For one, this may mean looking at the realities of implementation. A given idea about controlling online activity—maybe against trolls and other troublemakers—might be appealing, but how would it work? Who would be in charge? Who would be overseeing whomever is in charge?

Tied in closely with this is the problem of policy enforcement. If a drug policy requires active checks, what kind of a logistical lift would be involved in officers performing those checks? If they're random or limited in scope, would there be potential for bias in selection?

Another possible concern is the scalability of a given solution. Maybe something has shown promise in a smaller country, or on a local level. What would be the costs of scaling it up? Would equipment and training have to be provided to those enforcing—and if so, what would that entail? If it's something with a proven track record in urban settings, would it work in rural ones?

Wherever we look, there is more to dig and dive into, widening the toolset for thoughtful and informative discussion. Of course, we don't have to reach any formal solution—we're not lawmakers here—but by playing this role, we can cultivate an intellectual humility essential for any future discussion, and for life beyond politics as well.

Don't Depend on Doctrine

All this talk of efficiency, effectiveness, and propensity to error may seem technical to some. It might be well suited for certain economic topics, but how can it be satisfactory when looking at the moral crises of our time?

I promised at the start that I would not ask readers to abandon any deeply held convictions, and I won't. When adding these considerations to the policy puzzle, however, it does help to create a bit of distance. This is to say, morality should very much factor in—but it's not the morality of you as (would-be) policymaker that matters.

Rather, it helps in cases like these to understand ourselves as voices of a greater moral outcry. This outcry, regardless of the particular ethics of any policymakers, should represent a significant societal concern, and a clear cause for legal action or change.

Is there, for instance, any purely utilitarian case against the recreational torture of animals? Perhaps, to some degree, in the form of psychological impacts, particularly on troubled minds. By and large, though, it is the sort of activity we have banned because a great many people would find it appalling. And that is reason enough.

A demoralized population is one prone to unrest, prone to be less productive and less positively engaged. It is a thing worth looking to prevent, and for this reason—though it may not necessarily trump other considerations—it leads us to respect any great outcry, even when the sentiment isn't our own.

> We've become deeply accustomed to the rhythm of politics inside of our bubbles. The words we use, the emotions and the values we appeal to, speak to what affirms and energizes us. This style isn't well suited to attract outside audiences, because that's not what it was ever intended for.

Many values appeals—which otherwise might not feel so universally accessible—can be worked into this framing: the plight of the homeless or the uninsured or the undocumented, public worry about crime or government overreach or indoctrination, and so forth. Some of these moral concerns will be double-sided—abortion policies, for one, tend to be appalling to a segment of the population however they read—but even in these cases, it allows us to better consider these perspectives in a cohesive conversation.

The crucial point is this: **the basis of your argument determines the reach of your argument.** If all your conclusions are built upon a moral assertion, then those who don't share that assertion will struggle to understand what follows. Finding ways to overcome this, and to communicate your points and concerns without relying on an acceptance of doctrine, without having to agree perfectly on some situational assessment, can empower you to reach those you may have thought unreachable, on topics you may have thought impossible to discuss.

Appreciate the Issue at Hand

The frameworks covered in this chapter are meant to be broad and flexible, in order to approach a wide range of topics—if they weren't, that would obviously limit their usefulness. But for as much as I may like to leave it there and make things more open to interpretation, it helps to examine the most popular and pressing issues, and how the ideas and language that I've presented can be applied.

The following is, as so much of this book, based upon the time of writing in the U.S., but I hope that it holds some applicability wherever and whenever readers may see to utilize it.

This is by no means a complete list. These examples, however, focusing mainly on hotter-button topics, may serve well to better illustrate the range of discussions that a common language can help facilitate.

Finally, you may also not always agree with my interpretation and assessment. Of course, it's difficult to put aside my biases completely. As with the issues themselves, things are complicated, and I look forward to seeing others' interpretations of how these tools might be applied.

Abortion / Reproductive Rights—Many partisan interpretations view this topic as very much black-and-white: either life begins at conception, and abortion is essentially murder, or any significant restrictions upon reproductive rights are a violation of bodily autonomy and the human rights of women. I am not going to attempt to refute or dissuade the reader from either viewpoint, but I will suggest a few pathways to avoid a loud moral argument where no one is likely to budge.

If we look from the perspective of a society dealing for decades with clashing moral outcries, the complexity of the issue starts to become apparent, and from this angle, we can start to think more collaboratively. If we have the right mindset, of course.

"What works" is a complicated question, but it's not as unanswerable or subjective as one might think. You may ask, for instance, how effective abortion bans are at reducing the number of abortions, when accounting for under-the-table procedures, out-of-country actions, and the difficulties of tracking illegalized activity. You might ask how effective state and local bans can be, and which cases would be most significantly impacted.

Moreover, there may be some common ground to be found in focusing on minimizing the situations which might lead to an abortion decision, as the associated experiences can be traumatic. This is a line of thinking that can resonate even with a more pro-choice audience, and can lead to (hopefully productive) discussions around effective sex education, assurances around resources and financial support, and even crime law. There's more common ground to be found than you might expect, but again—most of us aren't used to looking for it at all.

Climate Change / Environment—Speaking for myself, I find the discourse around the environment, particularly since the early aughts, to be among the most frustrating topics to hear discussed. It is needlessly polarized and contentious, marred by the way we imbue our egos into its discussion.

The way we're used to talking about climate change, those on the Left will typically insist that their opponents accept what they see as the science and the expert analysis on the subject. Those on the Right will often fixate on the infeasibility of certain measures, the exaggerations or misses of past climate predictions, or what they view as hypocrisy among climate change advocates or their blindness to policies' cost. In either case, it is a mindset focused on making the other admit defeat in some way. As such, it is not only aggressive and unlikely to be well received, but it also drives us, in turn, to be more defensive and emotionally charged on the subject, which may invite abuse—by special interests looking to undermine calls for action, profiteers and virtue-hoarders looking to play upon panic, or both.

All the while, there's actually a great deal of common ground available around cleaner air, cleaner water, and generally more sustainable environmental policy as worthy goals in themselves. How to make that viable and workable, however, is not a simple problem in the face of industry realities and immediate energy needs. And it's a problem better solved together.

There are indeed ineffective, untenable, or destructive policies that can be created in the name of positive climate action. If you're an advocate for greater action and reform, this is not something that should be downplayed or hidden—acknowledging this is an invitation for thoughtful feedback, a gesture of intellectual humility that can go a long way.

And if you're pushing for more skepticism, you absolutely can and should bring up these potential excesses, but it's crucial not to be dismissive in doing so. If you seek not only to criticize but to help refine—to imagine policy that is more scalable, more efficient and effective, and even more politically viable—then your partner in conversation is going to be far likelier to listen.

Crime / Criminal Justice—We do not all share the same sense of justice. We just don't. What we think someone might deserve for a given offense may vary wildly, and we might not even agree on what constitutes a crime at all. And yet, the opportunity for a collaborative discourse is still present if we just try to think about what works.

To understand this idea here is to think critically about laws' effectiveness as deterrents and safe-keepers for the public, about our justice system's capacity for and effectiveness in reforming criminals and preventing recidivism, and about the costs our criminal policy—both in terms of the financial toll of mass incarceration, as well as the human costs of lost opportunity (among the punished, but among victims too) and the cycles of poverty or trauma to which they might contribute.

At the same time, however, if you feel that some punishments or lacks thereof are morally repugnant, remember you are likely not alone in your moral outcry, and that a common feeling of injustice happening is a societal ill in itself. Criminal policy seen as objectionable, by extension, is going to be less sustainable as policy, and this is something we can point to, even while speaking with those who lack our own sense of justice.

Foreign Policy / War—When we talk about war, we typically focus on who and what is justified, on past transgressions and consequences owed. These are topics on which we are inevitably going to disagree often, and quite fervently when we do.

Instead, it may help to focus on where things are going, and how problems are ultimately solved or perhaps worsened through conflict. What does "winning" for a given side accomplish, and what does it look like? What will happen or be achieved if we or some other nation should try to avoid or delay conflict?

Gender Issues / Trans Rights—Here we have another case of potential error and misuse of policy, that is sometimes very difficult to see as such because of the assumptions we tend to bring into the discussion.

When we look at laws around gender identity and how one can change it, for instance, many will focus solely on those with the best of intentions looking to these laws for a needed sense of affirmation. Many others, meanwhile, will focus only on those being misguided or misinformed in their assessment of their own identity, or on those who would abuse maliciously whatever the laws allow, who would lie to get favorable treatment, advantages in work or sport, or whatever the case may be.

The reality is that both cases are possible, and both need to be accounted for—that is, yes, people can have the best of intentions, or they can have the worst. To speak in absolutes about the trans community, or to assume intent, is to add personal judgments to what is already a deeply emotional issue for many.

Even if the likelihood of abuse of a policy seems low, we need to consider it and the incentives it may create. And even if the case of harm through a policy being or not being in place seems unlikely, we need to consider it and the risk of human loss (in terms of demoralization, depression, or worse) it may entail. By looking through this lens, we can reinforce the need to hear each other, and through this, we can better listen, and ultimately better feel a part of a conversation.

There are other issues that fall under this label as well, including questions around harassment and how it can be controlled, and around competitive sports and their participants. In all of these cases, however, the question of how well policy works can serve us well in driving toward healthy conversation.

Guns / Gun Control—This one's all about power and its possible abuses. The individual with access to guns can do so many things, while the state or legal enforcement denying this access—to whatever extent—has its own potential for overreach. Logistics are complicated, from accounting for illegally present weapons, to trying to plan out and enforce registration systems or buyback programs. Add in evolving technology and a major mental health crisis, what may have been effective policy before may not necessarily be so now.

In short, it's complicated. But it helps to take the societal perspective of trying to build effective policy while maintaining a healthy system of checks and balances, if for no other reason than to allow us to feel like we're hearing each other.

Immigration—Here's another complicated issue, which astute readers might notice is getting to be a bit of a trend. Functional immigration policy needs to take a lot into consideration when it comes to the realities of immigrants' situations, and the realities of what a change in policy might do, factoring in the incentives laws may create for current and potential migrants. There are plenty of knobs to turn, from quotas and amnesties to various border control and enforcement measures.

But beyond all of this, the case of immigration is perhaps the clearest example of why we need a healthy, problem-solving-focused discourse on a macro level. Inconsistent policy creates instability at our borders and terrible uncertainty for immigrants, leading to constant chaos as our problems remain unresolved. Given the way partisan tides turn, however, any long-term policy would require extensive collaboration, collective thought, and well-informed compromise.

All of this should give us good reason to at least try our best to view the issue with open minds and analytical eyes. And while we may only be modeling it in our conversations with friends, family, and neighbors (for now), it's a valuable and fulfilling exercise nonetheless.

Labor / Wages—Questions around labor involve complex power structures in need of careful balancing. This power can be found in corporations, their government oversight, in unions and their individual member or nonmember workers, and in the legal systems and tools these various parties can employ. And because this is an economic system, any potential abuse of power—if profitable—can be especially dangerous.

Some may point to massive corporations being responsible for a great many of these abuses, and the point is valid. Rather than point the finger at corporate greed, though, it may help us in our discussions to realize that any imbalance of power is ultimately a policymaking failure as well. By shifting focus this way, we can avoid the tension and hostility of class division (which also makes our conversations deeply unproductive) and unite against the common enemy of bad policy.

Policing / Police Reform—Here, we have another question of abuses of power, which people recognize as a question of abuses of power, and yet it remains a hot button difficult for many to navigate. Why? Because it highlights starkly the fear and the outrage that can come with being on the wrong end of a potential power imbalance.

When these issues are most present in the public conscience, we tend to focus on the particulars of the most recent allegations of injustice, and, as always, this leads to a lot of conversations that don't go very far. It helps to instead think about the systemic checks and balances in play, and what happens when something goes wrong. How do we oversee the police, and how can this oversight be as incorruptible as possible without undermining important work? How can we effectively minimize error and avoid dangerous situations, while mitigating the harm done by any individual who should abuse their power?

Voting Access / Voting Integrity—Finally, we arrive at a contentious topic at the heart of some of the most dangerous and consequential moments in our partisan strife. And yet, it's a fairly basic balance-of-power issue.

Can making voting too easy—through online or mail voting, absentee ballots, more lax ID checks, and the like—create the potential for abuse and error? Yes, absolutely, and this should be considered. Can making voting too difficult—through tests and more stringent verification checks—create the possibility of abuse via enforcement, and create issues for some who should be allowed rightfully to vote? Yes, of course, and these points should be considered in policymaking as well.

Leave the Door Open

By now, hopefully, the applications are becoming somewhat easier to find, and, again, the above is far from a comprehensive list. It will, in fact, never be a comprehensive list, and it shouldn't be. There's always going to be more insight one can add—this is the beauty of a curious mindset.

This openness to input and interpretation is essential to both healthy discourse in the societal sense, and healthy conversations in the personal. It is part of what creates the essential feeling of empowerment and encourages engagement. Without it, we would be subject to the whims of bureaucrats, technocrats, or AI.

And as much as we may want to have the last word, this urge runs counter to a healthy and welcoming discourse. Ideas can always be questioned and improved, and as denizens of a democracy, we have no lawmaking deadlines. Besides, our partners in conversation might like to have the last word too, and we can't both have it, can we?

It's better this way. Establishing a common political language takes time, and the conversation that follows should continue to grow, welcoming more and more voices and ideas into its fold.

9

Toolboxing

Fostering an Additive Conversation

I n 2019, tech entrepreneur and political newcomer Andrew Yang
made his bid for the Democratic nomination for the following year's
presidential contest. Though he wasn't ultimately nominated, his campaign defied odds and made national waves, headlined by his trademark
issue of universal basic income. And yet, would you believe that only
some 60% of Yang's *own supporters* stood with him on this signature
topic?

Having myself worked with Yang and his gang by way of his later
efforts with the Forward Party, I was privy to some of his team's discussion around that number, and why it was so surprisingly low. According
to their internal polling, it seemed that those voters who supported Yang
despite disagreeing with his UBI stance were simply impressed that he
was thinking about the issues that a changing industry landscape would
bring, that he was trying hard to address the potential tumult of shifting
opportunities. In other words, what mattered to them was that he was
asking the right questions, even if they didn't feel he had the right answer.

Is there a right answer? We often assume that there should be, but
there are so many things to consider, from the costs involved with any
particular approach, to the nuances of implementation and enforcement, to the society's response and behavior in the face of new policy.
Not all of this can be easily gauged, and even if we were to factor every-

thing in, we might end up with a handful of paths to choose from, each offering some set of tradeoffs to assess.

It's a daunting journey, to say the least, but it starts with putting ideas on the table. Every proposal and perspective allows us, as those trying to think about the problems, to get a slightly clearer view of what it is we can do. Through these ideas and our assessments of them, we can begin to understand what tools we have to work with in facing any given problem. If we appreciate this, then it should follow logically that new ideas, new voices, and new perspectives should be welcomed, and indeed celebrated. By applying this thinking to the common discourse—that is, people just talking about the issues rather than those elected and tasked to solve them—we can open the door to a far more positive, dynamic, and intellectually stimulating political experience than we might be used to.

By embracing the toolbox—the understanding that every new idea is additive to a set of possible solutions—we can enjoy debates and conversations that are more exciting, more engaging, and, ultimately, more empowering.

Unsexy Problems and Unsimple Solutions

In the previous chapter, I talked about ways to approach the so-called "hot button" issues—abortion, guns, immigration, war, and so forth. These issues seem to be all the rage because, well, they inspire all the rage. They elicit deeply emotional responses, they divide us neatly into opposing camps, and they allow us to be absolutely certain that we know where the answer lies on sheer moral principle.

There is another class of issue, however, that doesn't induce such partisan excitement. We might refer to this class as "cold button" issues—lower-profile and complex topics, often linked to economics, that don't generate headlines but nonetheless affect millions. Examples range from mitigating risk in global supply chains, to anticipating waves of immigration and displacement, to dealing with a growing mental health crisis among our younger generations. A number of these topics are seen as high priorities by the general population, but in the absence of easy answers, many—and particularly politicians and media—have little to say.

In 2024, I worked with a candidate for the Florida State House, who ran with property insurance as a headline issue. Costs had been spiraling over recent years—due in part to a run of destructive hurricane seasons—making it a top concern in polls not only in her district but all across the state. And yet, a strategist advised her not to focus so much on the topic because, as he put it, it was an "unsexy" issue.

To the strategist's point, these are the kinds of topics that mainstream candidates and media tend to avoid. There's no easy solution to sell, there's no "rah-rah" to inspire, and you can only get so far off sheer principles and moral declarations. Moreover, because these issues aren't as divisive as others, they don't give partisan candidates a clear shot at planting their flag and differentiating themselves. In an age where emotion and energy are the coveted currency of the political arena, it's understandable why many would stay away.

Fortunately, we don't have this problem in day-to-day discourse. We as individuals have neither the elections to win nor the public reputations to uphold, and this frees us to embrace the

difficulty and complexity of these problems. And because the conversation that would follow so clearly highlights the need for intellectual humility and collaborative discourse, we absolutely should be bringing these topics up.

> By embracing the toolbox—the understanding that every new idea is additive to a set of possible solutions—we can enjoy debates and conversations that are more exciting, more engaging, and, ultimately, more empowering.

Working through complex issues leads us to a greater appreciation of nuance and a more curious mindset. Nobody has *the* answer, but each new voice and perspective inches us closer to clarity, to understanding what a solution might look like. Here, more than any other kind of political conversation, thinking differently helps.

This, in essence, is the beauty of Yang's approach, and why, I would contend, he managed to find the resonance he did with what so many viewed as an imperfect solution. Because universal basic income *is* an imperfect solution—it is simply an option for how to distribute wealth to incentivize positive economic behaviors. The same description might apply to any tax cut, or any welfare program. Each offers its own benefits—tax cuts put more spending power in the hands of individuals, welfare programs offer safety nets to those in the greatest need, and UBI offers generalized mobility and economic freedom. Each also has its own costs—tax cuts may underserve those who are struggling, and end up widening economic inequality, welfare programs may create adverse incentives or even contribute to cycles of dependency and poverty, and

UBI can be extremely costly and have inflationary effects depending on the scale.

Does this leave three imperfect options? No, in fact it leaves infinitely more, once we realize that each kind of program offers something of a knob to turn to any level we find appropriate. They're not mutually exclusive—a possible solution might include some tax cuts to bolster business while UBI offers a safety net, or a smaller UBI implementation with a welfare program to ensure security for those in greatest need, or some blend of all three.

This is what working with a toolbox looks like. We can combine ideas, we can adjust ideas, we can welcome in new ideas. The more we can see and consider, the more we're able to work constructively toward finding the best possible solutions.

Of course, depending on where we are and what we're trying to do, the solution we're looking for may vary quite a bit.

Putting Context in Matters

It's worth acknowledging at this point that many of the issues we face and discuss on a daily basis aren't federal, even if the federal ones seem to get the lion's share of attention. State and local policies can have significant effects on our lives and livelihoods, and in many ways work (not always effectively) to address the same things—needs for infrastructure, controls on guns, illicit substances, and various behaviors, and economic drivers and incentives, to name a few. Even when the questions appear similar, however, it doesn't mean the answers have to be the same.

There are starkly different realities in urban and rural living; realities which affect what kinds of infrastructure are needed, and which are going to be most useful. Different demographics may be reflected in demand for services, and in sentiments around cultural issues. And the scale, costs, and impact of any economic measures will vary wildly.

> We can combine ideas, we can adjust ideas, we can welcome in new ideas. The more we can see and consider, the more we're able to work constructively toward finding the best possible solutions.

Looking again at UBI and its alternatives, we can see the dramatic shifts in prospects depending on these contexts. A basic income implementation may have less inflationary risk and more of an impact on spending power when it's specific to a state or a locality. The same kind of tax cut may drive different behaviors depending on the local opportunities, and depending on whose gains actually translate into spending money. A targeted welfare or assistance program, meanwhile, may have its success depend upon the other factors contributing locally to poverty and need, and the new opportunities it might be able to open up.

All of this points to just how complex many of these issues are, but again, the problems being complex shouldn't mean we ought to give up on solving them. **It means that we should embrace the conversation.**

What works in one place may not work so well in another. What has succeeded abroad may not necessarily be so successful in the States, and vice versa. Each data point, each success or failure, is valuable, and everything adds to the discourse—as long as the discourse is additive.

Adjusting the Hat

A few chapters ago, I talked about rethinking the roles we play in conversation, from philosophers conceiving their perfect worlds to legislators tasking themselves—and each other—with doing the work to find solutions. Now, it's time to take the next step.

Rather than imagining ourselves as ultimate decision makers, instead we can see ourselves as inputs in this decision-making process, as something more along the lines of a think tank. We are brainstorming, doing our part to advise by gathering what ideas and information we have, and combining that with what we can learn from others.

The beauty here is it's no longer really pretending at all. We can share with others the ideas and solutions we come up with, and if they're good—if they're well thought out, well presented, and pertinent to the problems of the day—they can spread far and wide. Eventually, these ideas can develop into local policies, and if their implementations are promising, then they might be emulated in other localities, or on the state level, or on the national stage.

Even if our ideas don't make it all the way into law, there is still plenty to enjoy in the journey. Fostering a conversation where new ideas are welcomed can inspire problem-solving minds, can encourage healthy dialogue, and can make for a much better political experience.

The Power of the Toolbox

More than just being a welcoming experience, the toolbox approach to political thinking speaks to a different part of the brain than debate usually would, allowing us to imbue our dialogue with a sense of creativity and even wonder. **Maintaining civil discourse shouldn't feel like a chore**—this is why pathways to making it more enjoyable, more intellectually stimulating, and more empowering are so essential.

At its best, this approach and mindset can empower through an emphasis on individual voices in conversation, and not just team competition. Each one of us can shine by adding our unique ideas, perspectives, and experiences. We feel heard and valued, and we share the feeling with others as we welcome them in.

This framework also helps to humble us. The more we face complex issues and appreciate their complexity, the more we're able to embrace the collaborative approach to solving them, and to internalize why it's so important. As we hone that skill, it becomes easier and easier to apply and maintain this intellectual humility, to be patient and curious with differing voices—and hopefully, to pass the sentiment along.

If all of that sounds appealing, but you're finding it difficult to understand what applying such a framework to important issues would look like, a few examples might help:

The Issue: Poor Economic Activity—At the outset of this chapter, I brought up the case of UBI, and this is one way to understand the core issue that such a program would be trying to address. In a nutshell, the incentives aren't pointing where the society would want them to point, industry isn't growing, businesses are taking their business elsewhere, people aren't buying things, cash isn't flowing, and so forth.

The Toolbox: When the goal is to stimulate economic activity, tax cuts can address the issue by creating more spending power, particularly for higher earners, giving business leaders more freedom to innovate and expand. Welfare and aid initiatives can provide valuable assistance to those with the greatest need. UBI and stimulus programs provide more generalized spending power and risk mitigation, for both higher earners choosing to expand and hire, as well as lower earners looking to make a pivot or struggling to make ends meet. Each solution comes with its costs and potential drawbacks, and incentives and inflationary effects need to be considered carefully, but ultimately, some combination of these sorts of tools and programs—as well as, perhaps, a few not yet considered—can drive toward the activity we need.

The Issue: Cost of Living—Tied in closely with the above is a phrase bandied about heavily in the 2020s—and for good reason. From housing and rents, to gas and groceries, to insurance on everything that needs to be insured, this is the ultimate pocketbook issue and a frequent top-placer on priorities among the public. And while the individual costs can be addressed specifically through a range of policy measures, there's a common toolbox that may help us understand what we're dealing with.

The Toolbox: Aid programs, stimuli, and tax cuts can all bolster spending power, but each one has inflationary potential, which is especially dangerous here. Price controls and restrictions on corporate gouging can help to address concerns on the sellers' side, while industrial economic incentives and even public initiatives on things like infrastructure can assist by bolstering supply.

The Issue: Labor—We've touched on this before as a prime example of a complex power structure that needs to be delicately balanced. It fits into this framework just as well.

The Toolbox: Within such a complex power structure, the toolbox needed to maintain health and stability is essentially just the set of checks and balances applied to each player within the structure. Corporations are restricted in how they treat employees and unionization within their ranks, while unions are prevented from coercing laborers to join or engaging in otherwise anti-competitive practices. All of the parties involved, including the individual workers, have access to various means of legal recourse if another party infringes on their rights, and all of these means of legal recourse need to be kept in check in turn, lest they be used frivolously or otherwise abused.

The Issue: Education—What's this, a non-economic issue? Yes, and the toolbox framework can be applied here, as well. Once you realize that the quality of our education and the outcomes of our education come down to far more than how much money we put into these things federally, it becomes clear that this is a complex issue, and one which stands to benefit from a versatile set of potential solutions.

The Toolbox: Beyond funding hikes (or cuts) at the federal, state, and local levels, dynamic education policy can also feature voucher and school choice programs, as well as subsidies for private and higher education (which should be kept in check lest they lead prices to inflate beyond reason). On top of this, the content being taught can be guided through both public policy restrictions and grants and initiatives for new curriculum inclusions. Volunteer and service programs (such as Teach for America) can further enhance the educational experiences and ultimate outcomes for students, and can even become a manpower resource for more educational programming down the line. This list isn't comprehensive, of course, and more ideas should be welcome—including yours.

The Issue: Immigration—The toolbox framework can be applied even to seemingly the most polarizing issues—again, it comes down to appreciating complexity and realizing that meaningful, long-term solutions don't exist on a simple binary scale.

The Toolbox: Beyond quotas and more generalized approaches to legal inflows, policy should also—and does also—consider a wide range of visa programs that incentivize migrants with different skills and backgrounds to address different societal demands. On questions of illegal immigration, there are a variety of security measures that can be implemented, and effective implementation requires a careful assessment of logistics around enforcement, and a practical understanding of what means may be used to enter the country if some are blocked off. Amnesty programs offer a potentially powerful tool to reduce the logistical load and clear the situation, but using them repeatedly can distort incentives. All of this and more should be considered, and all while keeping in mind the benefit of consistency for stability, clarity, and peace of mind among those in the country and those looking to one day move.

The toolbox framework may not apply to every issue, but it might apply to more than you think. Particularly as we zoom out and assess the difficulties of effective policymaking in virtually anything, we can see complexity present in more and more issues that we may have previously thought of as binaries. We can understand guns through the frameworks of local controls, licensing processes and organizations and their over-sights; we can understand abortion through a broader lens that incor-porates safe sex programming, crime prevention, financial resources for young parents, and anything else which might affect the frequency of situations where an abortion would be considered.

When we stop to appreciate this sort of nuance, it allows us to experience politics differently. No longer is it just a matter of disagreeing civilly—in some cases, even in honest discussions with those who seem most diametrically opposed to ourselves, and even without bending on any of our beliefs, it can feel like we're not disagreeing at all.

The First Rule of Improv

If you enter into a conversation yelling about how the Other Side and everything that they support is evil, you're likely to be met with the Other Side yelling back. You'll have a hard time convincing anyone of your point, and you'll find little in the way of growth.

If you tone things down and lead with thoughts along the line of "I believe that we should adopt such-and-such a policy," then suddenly you might have a more workable conversation. You're more likely to be met with a response along the lines of well, I believe this," or "but what about..." You may not ultimately come to an agreement, but you might come to understand each other better.

Now, if you utilize the toolbox framework to take things a step further, you can embrace the part of the contributing thinker in the braoder discourse. You can lead with specific ideas and concerns, with your observations on a particular issue. Once your partner in conversation is used to the flow of things, they might reply with a "yes, and," followed by their own concerns and observations, which you can add together to gain a more cohesive view of the issue and a wider toolbox to draw from.

Astute readers may recognize this "yes, and" line as the trademark first rule of improvisational comedy. Though it's never spoken in performance, the line is a mantra that guides participants to adopt every added piece of information into the rhythmic flow of a scene. In much the same way, it can help us incorporate an ever-widening set of perspectives into our political thinking, and begin to build out thoughtful and productive discussions around it.

To see the kind of ideas we might deal with, let's examine once more the topic of business and labor, and its evolution through history. It begins, somewhat fittingly, in the Enlightenment Era, as the excesses of early corporations and the struggles of workers led to the idea of labor unionization. Amidst the Industrial Revolution, the largest corporations grew in power, and needed to be further checked with anti-trust laws. Later, the growing power of some unions would infringe upon the economic mobility and freedoms of individual workers, who would push to limit union power through landmark legal cases. The legal recourse individuals gained also had its potential for excess, which needed to be reined in by further policy, and all the while, corporations found new ways to leverage size and capital, which needed to be kept in check.

To be clear, this development of policy was not all done through friendly conversation—far from it. There were hard-fought legal, political, and even physical battles, and I mean to take nothing away from those who fought and sacrificed along the way.

By boiling this progress down to key breakthroughs, however, and by seeing how they relate to one another, we can better understand the essence of effective solutions in key matters. In turn, we can better realize what a collaborative problem-solving mindset can bring, and the conversations it can produce.

> **The more we face complex issues and appreciate their complexity, the more we're able to embrace the collaborative approach and intellectual humility needed to solve them.**

These are conversations that, at their best, are fundamentally additive—each new voice contributes positively toward the solution-building process. The Right checks the Left, watching over the excesses of oversight in defending the liberties of the individual. The Left checks the Right, watching for individual and corporate excess while defending the well-being of the greater public. Outside-the-box thinkers add creative and novel ideas to the toolbox. Mediating voices temper the emotions of the conversation and can guide toward critical compromise. Passionate advocates drive needed urgency and help ensure that the issue at hand receives the attention and priority it deserves. Together, all of these voices can be complementary, working toward something far greater than any could alone.

If we embrace the mentality of working to create such conversations, it can allow us to forge a relationship with politics that is happier, healthier, and more sustainable. And we can do this while simultaneously becoming more effective communicators and more capable advocates for the things we believe.

Win First, then Go to War

Though it will help you change minds and get your points across to new audiences, the toolbox framework is not just a recipe for victory. It is victory in itself.

The toolbox, after all, is the realization of a curious and collaborative mindset. It is the understanding that every conversation with someone of a different perspective offers an opportunity to better inform your ideas. Every conversation becomes additive, and each exchange of ideas brings us closer to better solutions.

The legendary strategist Sun Tzu wrote, "victorious warriors win first and then go to war, while defeated warriors go to war first and then seek to win." Here, you are the victorious warrior.

But wait, why are you a warrior at all? Why am I bringing up *the Art of War*? Isn't the whole point that we're not supposed to be thinking of politics in such competitive or combative terms as we're used to?

Well, yes and no. We shouldn't be at war with one another—and we don't need to be. We are at war, however, with the crises we face. Every day, lives are on the line, and incredible harm is done as we continue to lay trapped by our tribal divisions and the political theatre profiting off of them.

The challenge of communicating in the modern age with those of differing worldviews is one of our greatest obstacles. If we can overcome this challenge internally, before even stepping into conversation with others, then we indeed win a critical battle before it is fought, and prepare ourselves far better for the greater battle—against our societal ills—that lies ahead.

Eight Bedrocks of Better Discourse
Laying a Foundation with Guiding Principles

Before we move on to best practices for engaging others in constructive dialogue, and before we explore what it would take to viably bring a more positive ethos to our elected politics, it's time to put together what we've learned. It's time to summarize things in a way that is quick to read and convenient to reference. It's time, ladies and gentlemen, for a list.

The following is a set of foundational principles to take to heart and keep in mind as we work to engage in more productive dialogue with those who may not always share our views. Wherever you may find yourself on any political spectrum, whatever you're looking to bring to the table, these will empower you to engage in conversations that are healthier and more fulfilling. You will become a more effective advocate for your values and ideas, while at the same time making others feel themselves more heard and their own thoughts more welcome. It starts here.

1. Fight the problem, not your partner in conversation

The first step involves challenging our assumptions about what discourse should feel and sound like, and breaking away from the conflict mentality that so many of us carry into it. Those with whom we engage in everyday conversation are not our political opponents, nor our enemies in any real war. Treating such disagreement as reason to fight creates undue stress and often inspires others to harden their hearts and deepen their conviction in response. We gain nothing, and lose friends and sleep along the way.

Our partners in conversation are not the problem—the problem itself is. We have very real crises in our time, some of which are worsening by the day, and too many of which are costing lives and livelihoods as they persist. As members of a democratic society, our most effective recourse is not to panic but to work together, to learn from one another and constructively challenge one another in pursuit of a better tomorrow that we all ultimately want, even if our notions of what that tomorrow will bring may differ.

2. Seek to learn, not to win

Remember first the Golden Rule, and that what you bring to conversation is likely to be reciprocated. If you enter seeking to win an argument, you will have on your hands an argument, and your partner in conversation will have no interest in either losing or admitting defeat. What follows is exhausting, stressful, and almost never productive.

Instead, if we enter into discussion with curious minds and a genuine desire to better understand different points of view, we might see others—more than you might expect—follow toward positive and constructive dialogue. We appreciate learning from them, they (over time) come to appreciate learning from us, and suddenly we have on our hands a win-win.

3. Open your own mind before asking others to open theirs

Now, let's extend this Golden Rule ethos. We all have our beliefs and values. If we believe that our notions of a better tomorrow would contribute to making a better tomorrow (as we should), then we would, of course, want others to open their minds to our ideas. We must first ask ourselves, however, if we are willing to do the same in return.

This does not require you to be constantly changing your views—you won't. It requires only that you maintain a willingness to learn, grounded in a healthy intellectual humility.

No single one of us is the Bearer of Truth. No one owns all the answers—if we did, then our only reasons to engage in dialogue would be to lecture and scold. You can accept these things and still be confident in your voice and your ability to add to the conversation, and the conversation will be fuller and more fruitful when you do.

4. Avoid moral imperatives and declarations

Approaching dialogue with a collaborative and curious mindset goes a long way, but it does not go all the way. What we contribute to the conversation matters, and it is incumbent upon us to ensure that the things we say are driving consistently toward a productive exchange of ideas.

Much of the politics we're used to hearing comes in the form of loud assertions and grand declarations. These are great for riling up crowds and preaching to choirs, but they are far less effective at persuading those outside the ideological group. It is valuable, certainly, to share your own worldviews and why you feel the way you feel, but to state these as facts, without "I believe" or similar qualifiers, can make them come across as loyalty tests or empty ranting.

5. Guide toward the bigger picture

It may require a few steps to go from shouting declarations to thoughtfully analyzing issues and perspectives, but you now have tools to help build this bridge. We can level the field of conversation and welcome a range of worldviews by asking critical questions with genuine curiosity: *What should we do? How and how well will it work? Where is the potential for error or failure?*

Asking these questions leads us to a better understanding of the power dynamics and often twisted incentives that underlie any societal ill. We can shift from blaming each other for our troubles to blaming the failures of policy and policymakers, and eventually to understanding what better solutions would entail.

If we lose sight of the broader policy picture, it is all too easy to get stuck on details or on the news of the day. We often disagree on facts or clash about why something matters as much as we think it does, when we would be far better served by zooming out.

6. Treat complex issues as complex issues

Common discourse—the sort that pervades cable news soundbites and social media shouting matches—would have you believe that the issues are all simple, and the right answers are obvious unless you're brainwashed or a fool. The reality is, when you consider what it means for a solution to be both effective and viable, solving what ails our society is deeply complicated. But not only is it okay to acknowledge this when discussing our views, we are actually empowered to engage with others more productively by doing so.

Accepting that complex problems are complex reinforces the sense of intellectual humility that is so vital to healthy conversation. Beyond this, it also helps to instill the mindset that every new perspective and conceptualization is essential to understanding what solutions might work. Factoring in the contexts of federal and statewide and local implementations and what they individually demand, it becomes clearer that what we need is not some common-sense super-solver telling us what the right answers are, but a robust toolbox of ideas and perspectives, all welcomed into an additive and thoughtful conversation.

7. Embrace new perspectives to better inform your own

One of the most pernicious aspects of our bubbling as a society is our inability to welcome ideas that challenge our own. In some circles, breaking from ideological dogma is viewed as betrayal and blasphemy. Not here.

Embracing different ideas and perspectives allows us to challenge and test our own, to broaden our horizons, and to add to our own toolbox of what effective solutions might entail. Doing so consistently allows us to sharpen our ability to present our own ideas, and to hone our strengths as advocates and champions of our values and beliefs far more than we ever could have by being surrounded with agreement.

8. Enjoy the conversation, and pass that joy along

If you go into dialogue with a genuinely curious mindset and the tools to guide toward a productive exchange of ideas, you will win. You will win by gaining valuable insight into how others think, and by strengthening your understanding of your own ideas and how to present them. You will win every time.

The beauty here lies not only in this dialogue being more intrinsically enjoyable, but also in the attractiveness of such a thing to others. You need not lecture anyone about the virtues of civil and thoughtful discourse, when you can simply share the experience of becoming a more effective communicator through less stressful and more fulfilling conversations.

And... that's it. These are the key tools to help you foster better conversations and become a more effective communicator and advocate for what you believe in. Now, it's just a matter of what you do with them.

PART IV

Planting the Seeds

YOUR GOAL: Reach Out

So, now what?

If you've enjoyed the book so far, then hopefully you've picked up on some frameworks to better process political questions, to better engage as both an effective listener and as an advocate for what you believe. Now, does that mean you're free to prance about, flouting your systemic analyses and toolboxen with careless abandon? Well, yes, I suppose—I can't stop you, anyway—but I wouldn't recommend it.

These are indeed powerful communication tools, but they aren't necessarily optimal for every setting. In fast-paced or noisy environments, you may not have the time or space to steer things toward a collaborative mindset. When things are heated or your partner in conversation is particularly worked up around a topic, you may need to be careful with the words you choose. On most social media forums, any nuanced take tends to get lost in the noise, and the mindset of the most prolific posters may pose a problem.

Each situation is different, and the scenarios explored in the chapters ahead will highlight this. By and large, the frameworks we've explored are at their best when you're one-on-one with someone with whom you have some established personal relationship, where you're free to be a bit more patient and a bit more thorough. They also offer the greatest value over replacement when you're dealing with someone with whom you've struggled to communicate well about politics in the past. Yes, this may mean that curmudgeonly uncle, or your activist daughter-in-law, or the coworker you've been trying to avoid.

Do you owe it to them to try to have these hard conversations? Maybe. Maybe not. That's another question for the philosophers.

But you can. Yes, even if you find yourself appalled by their politics. Even if you struggle to understand how they can believe what they believe. Even if you think they lack common sense or empathy in the way they think about the issues. Well, maybe they do—but maybe you can do something about it.

I'm reminded of the best piece of advice my mother ever gave me. I was seven or eight, a petulant child a few years removed from having lost my father (more on that later). And in a moment when she could have easily dismissed my whining or threatened to punish me if I persisted, she didn't.

Instead, she told me that, if I carried on the way I was going—sad and angry, stubborn and entitled—people would understand. I had my built-in excuse. But if I did so, I would lead a far less happy life for it, and I would be doing myself a tremendous disservice.

It's a nugget of wisdom not without its limitations—choosing to be happy isn't always as easy as it might sound, and sometimes it helps to process emotions by letting them out a bit. But for me, in that moment, it was the most powerful piece of advice I could have possibly received, and I will always be thankful for it. I hope it can be of some use to you.

So please, as you explore the scenarios and techniques laid out ahead, I encourage you to consider whom you might want to reach out to in your life. **Not because they deserve having you reach out, but because *you* do**. Because you can enjoy more positive and fulfilling conversations. Because you can grow together as communicators and political thinkers. Because the feeling of breaking through, especially when you've worked so hard for it, especially when you thought it might never be possible, is what makes it all worthwhile.

10

The Power of the Power of Persuasion

Satisfying Egos to Spread the Word

Why are we arguing, again?

No, no—I'm not asking why we care enough to argue. This we've discussed, and there are plenty of valid reasons why we care (along with a few dubious ones). The issues, frankly, are important to us. When we deem the stakes at hand to be existential, when we view our values and our principles and sometimes even ourselves or our loved ones under attack, it makes sense that we would have a deep investment in what happens.

There is a difference, however, between feeling compelled or justified in arguing passionately about something, and ultimately choosing to do so. All too often, I hear pleas for civility which frame fighting, yelling, and insulting as things we don't need to be resorting to, as if they're some extreme measures to be saved for dire situations. **All of that misses the point, however, that as a persuasive technique they profoundly do not work.**

Having an emotional response is natural. When we care so deeply about an issue, we begin to imbue it with our ego—our sense of identity, our sense of esteem and worth, even our sense of purpose and self. The ideas and opinions we hold intertwine with our values, representing what we believe not only about politics but about ourselves. The battle is not just something we are a part of—it is our own. If we can get others to admit some sort of defeat, then we are champions of our cause. It gives us an affirmation that we are right to believe what we believe so strongly.

What we are inclined naturally to do, however, is not necessarily what is effective in a civilized society. What comes across as hostility tends to be met with hostility or avoidance—that is, people not wanting to engage at all—and neither fight nor flight tends to result in anyone changing their mind.

We end up unable to make our point while being so invested, and this inability invokes a sense of failure and doubt. In protecting our egos, we are all too often eager to dismiss these moments as the Other Side's obstinacy, calling them brainwashed or delusional. Most dangerously, this inability to break through can contribute to a greater sense of isolation, to the notion that people aren't listening to us, won't listen to us, and don't want to hear what we have to say.

How we fare in political discussions matters to us, and it should matter. Strange as it may seem, I would root for any reader to experience changing someone's mind, if for no other reason than the sense of fulfillment and affirmation that comes with it. I do believe you deserve it.

So I would ask again, what are we arguing for? What does it accomplish? If we can save nerves and at the same time become better messengers for our cause, why wouldn't we?

Throughout this book, I have argued that a curious, analytical, and collaborative mindset not only makes our conversations more bearable, but also makes us more effective messengers of our beliefs and our ideas. Just as I offer this power of persuasion to you, you too can offer it to any partner in conversation, to help them engage more positively, and to encourage them to listen more to others.

The greatest breakthroughs come—in political dialogue or otherwise—when we are able to put ourselves in others' shoes. If you feel like your partner in conversation isn't "getting it," or isn't able to break out of unhealthy habits, **don't focus on the problems this creates for you.** Rather, consider theirs—they aren't able to communicate effectively outside their bubble, they aren't going to be able to break through to the people they would want to break through to, and they aren't going to become the best advocates they could be for their values and ideas.

Building Strength by Exposing Weakness

Once again, I go back to a debate I attended years ago, where participants were asked if America was the greatest country on Earth. At some moment during the event, a college-aged activist, speaking on the question in the negative, was asked what he would point to as an example of a great country. He named Cuba. A few in the audience audibly scoffed or laughed. The speaker was flustered.

I didn't get a chance to talk to the kid myself, but I thought about the statement for the rest of the night. I thought about how, if I or someone else had tried to argue with the statement itself, he would simply have gone into a defense mode, and the discussion would devolve quickly into which data sources to trust and so forth. Were I to have addressed the persuasiveness of the argument, however, and how jarring it tends to sound outside of a college activist bubble, he might have been more inclined to listen.

Now, did I feel I owed this to the individual? Not really. But maybe, if he were encouraged in a positive way to explore other perspectives, he might expand his horizons and reexamine some of his views. Maybe, if I were able to engage him as a partner in constructive conversation, I might learn more about his outlook and worldview, and even how I might make my ideas appeal more to such a mindset.

In cases like these, even if you should find yourself baffled, befuddled, or appalled by what you're hearing, it is possible to turn this into an opportunity to steer the conversation toward something more civil and more productive. **By focusing on the resonance and persuasiveness of an argument rather than its factual accuracy (which can be argued ad infinitum), you can get through to people you may not have thought reachable, and you can encourage them to embrace a better way of thinking about politics altogether.**

Paying it Forward

In driving toward healthier and more constructive dialogue, the draw of being a more effective messenger can be one of the most important tools in your belt. Simply *telling* others that they can be more persuasive, however, is not always enough—you'll want to show them what they can sound like if they adopt a more collaborative approach, and why it's so potentially powerful.

This means sharing all of the ideas covered to this point, from why it's so vital to be working toward a common goal, to the value of intellectual humility, to the power of the toolbox in discourse. It means sharing the idea of a common language, of the frameworks that can allow us better to understand each other. In passing this along, though, there is also an essential personal touch you can add.

Let's say, for instance, that the issue at hand is guns—you're broadly in favor of preserving gun owners' liberties, while your partner in conversation is more in favor of stricter regulations. Again, rather than focusing on what you disagree with or don't like in the arguments you hear, you can take a half-step back and point out what might not resonate with others on your side—perhaps the control policies they were suggesting might not make sense to those in a rural setting. Perhaps they were citing an author seen as particularly extreme by much of the Right, whose mention would be off-putting to such an audience.

Likewise, be sure to highlight things they do well. Perhaps they mentioned a statistic that you hadn't heard before, and you don't expect that many others would have. Perhaps they framed an argument in a way you found interesting or novel, that you think might also strike a chord with others.

It's all the same if the sides of the issue are reversed, or if the issue is health care, war, inflation, or anything else. If you help guide whomever you're talking to toward being the best messenger they can be, and if you can convey that you are putting genuine thought into your observations and trying to put yourself as much as possible in their shoes, then you can profoundly shift the tone of the conversations you have, and your efforts will not go unnoticed.

All of this might seem wildly counterintuitive if you're accustomed to a competitive approach to discourse. **The reality, however, is that the people in our lives we talk to about the issues are not our enemies.** We are not competing for any elected office, or over the approval of some neutral audience. We are, by and large, trying to build the best future and the best democracy possible. This, of course, is a task best undertaken together.

To this end, it is in your best interest to refine your ideas and test their mettle as much as possible. By allowing them to challenge you and provide their honest feedback, you can make whatever it is you want to say clearer, more resonant, and more compelling. Having more conversation partners who will challenge you with new perspectives is a massive asset in making your message the best it can be.

Of course, all of this applies to the people you interact with, too. Encourage them to refine their own ideas, to build them up as you build yours. The more they sharpen their iron, the better it can sharpen yours.

> By focusing on the resonance and persuasiveness of an argument rather than its factual accuracy , you can get through to people you may not have thought reachable, and you can encourage them to embrace a better way of thinking about politics altogether.

The deeper we go into this, the more we can unlock one of the great boons of pursuing persuasion. That is to say, the more we seek to become effective messengers, the more this journey will drive us to listen and learn from others, and to consider differing perspectives. It allows us to better internalize the tenets of a curious and open mind, and drives us toward interacting in a positive, productive, and symbiotic manner with others.

So keep challenging yourself with new ideas and new voices, and encourage others to do the same. It is through this process that we can best understand how to express ourselves and how to formulate our ideas. Eventually, some of those ideas might even make their way up toward real policy—though maybe not all of them.

Facing Fringes with False Flags

It should be acknowledged, of course, that not every idea will fare equally in the face of criticism, or in a more open marketplace of discourse. When we deal with the fringe, or what and whom we see as being on the fringe, this is something that needs to be taken into account, and a few targeted techniques may apply.

Broadly, extreme or fringe beliefs—wilder conspiracy theories and the like—have, by their definition, rather limited appeal. And because holders of these views tend to be rather entrenched in their beliefs, focusing on this—their limited ability to reach the audience they might want, and how it can be improved—may be far more effective than trying to prove to them that they're wrong.

For instance, let's say you have a friend who seems certain that the global elites are, in fact, Lizard People, headquartered at a secret base on the moon. Your first instinct may be to scoff at the idea, but you can instead step back and point out that many others would disregard the notion and the notioner. In turn, you can guide the individual toward ways to speak to the core of their belief—in this case, something along the lines of the powerful few in society being deceitful and disconnected from the many—in a way that might get more people to listen.

In offering something constructive, the sort of response such an individual may not be used to, you can direct your partner in conversation away from a defensive and paranoid mindset, and crucially lower the temperature of the discourse. In time, you can not only provide the experience of a productive conversation but the tools to engage in such a thing more often.

If you want, however, there is a way to take the argument one step further. Do use this reasoning sparingly, and please do so with caution.

Assuming that there *is* some conspiracy of elites afoot, you can explain that the Lizard People theory would be exactly how those elites would want their critics characterizing them, precisely because of the limited reach of the notion. After all, it makes the criticism sound unserious to many ears, and may even undermine the credibility of the critic and of more serious arguments against the problem at hand. In other words, the conspiracy theory itself *is* the conspiracy!

You may want to stop short of making an accusation—unless you have good reason to believe it—but pointing out who stands to gain the most, from an argument backfiring or sounding silly, can be eye-opening.

All this is not to say that any of these ideas are clearly or definitively wrong. This is not a presumption we should go into any argument with—if we're already certain they're wrong, after all, why should they offer us any kind of consideration? Opening minds to other perspectives (or at least, not dismissing those perspectives offhand) can be invaluable toward building the kind of discourse we need, while helping these more extreme thinkers feel heard—especially as they tend to be some of the most isolated and alienated in our society—can go a long, long way.

In Defense of the Ego

Throughout this chapter, I've talked quite a bit about appealing to the ego, and it's time to talk about what that really means. For many of us, hearing this word—*ego*—conjures the sour tastes of vanity and self-obsession, but it is far more than these connotations make it out to be.

Yes, the ego is at the core of some of the most toxic features of politics and discourse today, from zealotry and hostility to outright violence. It is at the core of demagoguery, of manipulation, of power-madness and megalomania.

The ego, however, is also essential in driving us to do good, and even to be good people. It is how we want to see ourselves, after all, that makes us so keenly aware of the shortcomings in our character and our accomplishments, and that makes us strive for better and more.

Beyond all of this, the ego is simply there. It is not something we can erase, or crush without doing tremendous harm. What we can do is work with it, work through it, and make the most of it.

Before my foray into politics, I spent a fair deal of time in the world of chess education. There, it is fairly well understood that ego and competitive drive are what get players interested in the game and eager to improve, by way of the thrill of victory and the trophies and praise that accompany it. For teachers and programs, the challenge is directing students through this toward consistent study habits, positive behavior, and a healthy competitive mindset, all while satisfying the sense of accomplishment that the kids came for in the first place.

It's not so different here. We want to validate our beliefs and be champions of our causes, to be the principled thinkers we aspire to be. **We can make our politics healthier and better, but this will only be scalable if doing so can offer the same appeal to our sense of self.**

So just as more divisive content found its greatest success by appealing to partisan egos, the greatest appeal of constructive discourse may be found in offering the sense of self-worth and power that comes with changing a mind, healing a relationship, and generally being heard.

Yes, the ego can drive us to harm, or it can motivate us to do incredible good. But we can have control of what direction it is pulling us in, if we first take the time to consider how it affects us and our own thinking.

A healthy self-awareness helps us put things in perspective, and to develop greater confidence and resilience. It is when we understand our ego that we can become the best versions of ourselves, and the best advocates of what we believe and what we stand for.

Eventually, when we do present the kind of captivating message that makes others stop and think, that's something we're going to be proud of, and we should be. It's a joy worth sharing.

11

Room for Exclusion

The Limits of Better Discourse

P icture yourself, a few weeks from now. You've made strides in internalizing a healthier political mindset. You understand the frameworks that empower positive and productive discourse. And yet, as you try to apply this all to conversation, you find in some places that people just aren't receptive. So, what are you doing wrong?

The answer, quite often, is nothing. Yes, these can be powerful tools for better conversation. This does not mean, however, that they always will be—**there are times and places where pursuing civil and analytical discourse won't yield the best results**. Rather than view this as a reason to give up, it is far better to take the time to understand why.

Matters of Place

A patient and analytical approach to discourse is not going to work in every setting, and there are some where it would likely fail spectacularly. The latter group tends to consist of places where conversation moves fast and people talk over one another. This might include a holiday dinner table debate with a lot of family members involved, an argument in a pub, or, most typically, an online forum or thread.

There are some wonderful exceptions around the web, with thoughtful discussions and analyses happening on every political topic—hopefully, the number might grow from this book and other calls for better discourse. More often, though, the political talk happening online tends to feature a lot of name-calling, a lot of straw-manning, and a lot of anger. If you try to incorporate some thoughtfulness and nuance, you may often find yourself drowning in the noise and becoming frustrated.

These are settings, after all, which lend themselves naturally to fiery, punchy, fast interactions. They are a major reason why this sort of dialogue is as prominent culturally as it has become, and why more pragmatic voices often find themselves pushed to the wayside. Passion and energy *work* online, and denying this doesn't get us anywhere.

This is not to say that trying to come in as a voice of reason would never work. Indeed, it might be possible to strike upon some breakthrough by chiming in to put different perspectives into a common context, or by helping other posters express their thoughts more persuasively. All of this depends, however, on the availability and interest on the part of other posters to engage further in such a conversation.

Put simply, a number of participants in the world of online politics are just looking to troll. Maybe they enjoy provoking a certain response, or love getting certain groups riled up. Maybe it's something of a game, something to provide a momentary rush of power and control, or perhaps some kind of catharsis for their personal frustrations.

Regardless, these individuals, not looking to engage in any good-faith conversation, are scattered all throughout the internets. Behind the wall of online anonymity, it can be difficult to gauge who's who, and you may find yourself expending a fair bit of time and energy before you realize a troll is a troll.

Likewise, many of those who do post in good faith may be wary of someone coming in and trying to engage them in deeper conversation. They might wonder, *Why are you asking all these questions? Why do you care so much about these framings, or how some phrasing might come across? Are you genuinely curious, or are you just trying to waste my time?* To them, you're hidden behind the same wall of online anonymity, and, for them, it's just as hard to tell.

Or maybe, they're simply in no mood to discuss.

The Hottest Buttons to Button

It's a sad irony that I've thought about more than once while writing this book: those with the most deeply held and cherished opinions are the ones who would benefit most from better conversational tools, and yet they tend all too often to reject the idea of a conversation altogether. The connection they have to their politics is too personal, with too many emotions involved. Sometimes in cases like these, the best course of action is to respect their views and move on.

Naturally, this will more often be the case with the classic "hot button" issues—abortion, guns, war, immigration, and anything involving children. These are issues, in our present-day understanding of them, that speak to the core of our moral compass, dealing with our most cherished values and freedoms and rights, our sense of autonomy and liberty and power. They are the wells of passion and emotion that fuel our modern political machines.

If you want to work toward a productive and open discourse around such issues, with someone who has deeply held beliefs, it'll demand a fair bit of effort. You'll want to establish a comfortable rapport, and make it abundantly clear that you're acting in good faith and want to help them better understand others' perspectives and communicate their sentiments to different audiences.

If you have some time to work with, you can try to ease in with some cooler buttons to establish tone and tenor, and to demonstrate frameworks of thinking about things. You can even start with non-political discussions, using those to model how a collaborative discourse can go, and how different perspectives can be productively shared.

Possibly the best tool for such a case is the ability to share a similar experience, if you've had similar deeply held beliefs, and learned over time how to better share them, discuss them, and have them challenged. Maybe this book helped with that (if so, hooray!), and you now have the opportunity to connect with others on a deep emotional level.

Whatever tools you're working with, if you try to rush or force open dialogue with someone who has no interest in engaging, you may offend them or even come off as a bully. You run the risk of damaging your relationship, and that's the opposite of what you should want these tools to be doing.

At the end of the day, some people simply don't care to debate certain topics, or have their most valued ideas questioned. Even presented with the prospect of becoming a better ambassador for their beliefs, they may prefer to just vent and speak their piece. And that's okay, too.

Playing the Other Game

One of the recurring themes throughout this guide has been that of flexibility—maintaining an open mind, considering different perspectives, and being ready to try varying approaches. As we extend this idea, however, we may find cases where the most effective approach may not be collaborative at all.

We've already discussed times where such an approach might not get through, or when your would-be partner in conversation doesn't want to engage at all. But there are also exceptional cases where another approach—perhaps a more standard approach—might simply work better.

Yes, minds do change, even in the current climate, and occasionally even through more combative means of discourse. As always, having an established relationship and rapport helps, and any precedent of changing minds after an argument is an indicator that they may be receptive to this sort of style.

It's also fair to observe a weak foundation as a sign of someone who might be swayed. If they base their conclusions on some misunderstanding (as you perceive it) of facts or on something that could be otherwise directly refuted, then by all means, go for it. There's still no need to yell or become aggressive—this is likelier to elicit a defensive response—but you can be direct.

Whatever approach you take, if your goal is to help someone open their mind to a different idea or a different perspective, it's going to take quite a bit of time to break through, even when the facts seem to be on your side. Breaking through in these situations can be immensely satisfying, but it is more than fair to consider the costs involved.

Matters of Time

Progress can be a slow process, and helping others to rethink the way they approach politics is absolutely no exception. Especially for those deeply engrained in their views and ideology, hearing about things like collaborative discourse or any of the tools above may be met with reticence or suspicion, and their tone isn't likely to change right away.

Now, it would be easy for me to declare that you should never give up, that you should persevere in every such case and use every tool and angle at your disposal. There is merit to this mentality, but there's also merit to valuing your time and your energy.

There are an infinite number of conversations you could be having, and an unimaginable number of people you could try to interact with and persuade. You can't reach everyone, and I hope you have other things to do with your life. Not every conversation needs to end with convincing someone to rethink their approach to politics.

You can, instead, save this determination for the conversations that really matter—for those close to you, for whom you might be their best chance to expand their horizons and guide them to a healthier mindset. If you can make even one or two of those partners in conversation feel heard, engaged, and empowered, that can make the entire journey feel triumphant.

12

Making It Personal

And Having Fun Along the Way

In 2024, shortly after the U.S. Presidential Election and on the eve of the Thanksgiving Holiday, a Harris Poll was released[1] that found that roughly half of the nation's adults were estranged from one or more immediate relatives or close friends. Political beliefs were not the cause of the majority of these estrangements—specific actions taken were the biggest culprit—but the 18% of these estrangements that were attributed to politics still account for tens of millions of Americans.

The idea that our political divisions could lead to more personal schisms isn't a new one, and this was far from the first evidence thereof. A 2020 Pew Center study[2] found that over 80% of Trump and Biden supporters had few or no friends who supported the other candidate—a product, in part, of greater regional and cultural political homogeneity, though the choices in friends we make and keep are sure to have played no small role. More recently, a survey by the dating app Hily[3] found that over 40% of women and more than 20% of men polled said they would never date someone who voted differently from them in the 2024 election.

Chances are, you have some relationships affected by differing politics in your own life. Maybe it's a complete estrangement of a once-close relative, or an otherwise solid friendship marred by occasional argumentative flare-ups. Maybe it's someone with whom these topics are left unspoken, for fear that disagreement would inevitably tear you apart.

Is every one of these worth fighting for? Not necessarily. There are plenty of toxic relationships in the world, people who bring stress into your life that you might be better off without. There are those whom you might never quite reach, and of course, there is the temptation to just leave politics undiscussed with certain people, and steer toward friendlier topics as much as you can.

What you have now, however, is a toolset you can use to mend, repair, or prevent these ruptures from happening. So, rather than needlessly accept another broken bridge, why not give dialogue a chance?

Putting It All Together

If I have done my job up to this point, then I hope that you feel better prepared to approach political conversation positively, to share your ideas constructively, and to engage with a broader range of voices. It follows naturally that you should also be better positioned to make others in your life feel heard and empowered to engage in discourse, but as we take this step, it may be worth reviewing what has been covered so far—and why it's important.

By now, you have seen the value of establishing a common goal and viewing politics through a collaborative lens. Through various frameworks and key questions, you also have the tools to put different issues into common context and language in pursuit of that shared objective.

I hope that you've also taken away the value of intellectual humility in welcoming others to engage in conversation and helping them take the first step in opening their own minds. Through the prospect of becoming a more effective advocate of one's beliefs, you can further attract these individuals to seeking out open and constructive discourse themselves.

Above all, I hope that you have been able to build some greater degree of self-awareness, to understand the nature of why we think and talk about politics the way we do. I hope that you have come to realize the senselessness of our constantly yelling at one another, and the beauty of approaching discourse with curious and open eyes.

> What you have now is a toolset for better understanding. Rather than accept another broken bridge, why not give dialogue a chance?

There is no script for sharing this insight with another, and I would caution against making any appeal seem rehearsed. **If you have gained from changing your mindset, then sharing that experience is the most genuine and the most powerful endorsement that you can give.**

Passing the joy along may take time. Growth may not be linear. Results are not guaranteed.

And yet, it remains an endeavor worth undertaking for its profound potential impact. For you, as the messenger, it can be the difference in maintaining a lifelong relationship and all you can gain and learn from that. For your partner in conversation, it can also mean a world of open doors.

Inlets and Outlets

It bears repeating, that the common ground that we're building isn't the things we agree on. It is the means by which we can engage with each other in healthy conversation, the arena in which we can effectively and productively *disagree.*

This distinction carries additional weight for those who feel unable to engage with some segment of our political population, or left out or turned away by our discourse altogether. The frameworks for talking politics with a broader audience are so essential here, not only because of the gateway they open to a larger conversation, but because of the space they create for you as an individual in that conversation.

That space is entirely your own. If we embrace the mindset that we gain from each unique voice, then it follows that you bring a value that only you can. You are the advocate only you can be, for your ideas, your perspective, and your experience. And if you should find yourself being a black sheep or a minority opinion, then, rather than be marginalized, you would in this sort of discourse become only more essential to the conversation.

In shifting focus to a broader conversation and our roles therein, it is moreover not only the outspoken who stand to benefit. There is value to be found in being a listener, in being a voice of moderation, in being someone with odd ideas that don't fit anywhere on a traditional spectrum of politics, or even in being formless and speaking for those unsure what to make of things.

All the tools shared here are designed to facilitate this broader conversation, and much of the benefit of doing so lies in our ability to invite people in. We can offer the same sense of community, purpose, and belonging as any other political tribe.

Only here, we can offer more than that. We can offer genuine positivity and hope in the face of a politics that is dreary and woeful. For young people who should engage, we can provide a sense of individual empowerment and fulfillment, and a sense of purpose that can yield benefits far beyond the political realm.

I'll go back again to my time teaching and promoting chess. In all of those years, chess was never the only game in town. It was, however, a pathway to challenge oneself, to explore and to grow, in much the same way that any other sport, or even competitions in arts or sciences, might offer. The children who pursued chess, however, were drawn to chess far more than any of these other options, and for them, having this particular pathway was a tremendous boon.

Political dialogue, at its best, can be much the same: a learning journey along which we can refine our ideas and hone our talking points by gathering data and hearing other perspectives. We may be challenged by those with whom we differ, or stumped by arguments we've not anticipated—yes, this is okay—but through it all, we gain insight and experience. If we persevere, we come out with a better understanding of ourselves and the world around us.

That this sort of thing would be beneficial for kids is neither shocking nor new. Arenas of civic discourse are open through Model U.N. teams and associations, as well as student governments that start in some places as early as the elementary level.

And yet, we would never think of talking politics as anything so positive. It could be an incredible outlet for fulfillment and intellectual expression, not only for adolescents but for anyone struggling to fit in and gain a greater sense of belonging. Instead, our modern discourse is toxic, miserable, and all too often performative—and, really, who wants to take part in that?

Politics Doesn't Have to Suck

You may have noticed that I'm prone to the occasional flight of whimsy. I'll use an odd turn of phrase here or there, or a punny chapter title, or an odd musical reference. I write that way because it's my voice, of course, but I leave it in with intention.

It doesn't mean I don't take political problems—or the problems with politics as a whole—seriously. I simply don't believe that we need to be gravely serious to solve them, and I would rather people hear what I have to say because it's pleasant to listen to, than that they would do so out of some forceful sense of moral obligation.

Political discourse is all too often humorless, and understandably so—lives indeed are on the line, and far too many have been lost and ruined because of bad policy and misguided or corrupt leadership. This is the reality of things. But while it may well justify panic and dread, do panic and dread really help solve the problems?

If we break it down, the self-seriousness of our politics is often built on faulty assumptions. We assume we need to be dreadfully serious to convey serious dread, but this doesn't really help our message. We view our own zealous declarations as signs of confidence, when so many roll their eyes at such things.

Moreover, **if the only draw of the political conversation is its direness, then a great many will tune out and continue tuning out.**

These impacts are seen in widespread pessimism about our political state and low turnout compared to other democracies, even when the stakes seem to be so astronomically high.

> Political dialogue, at its best, can be a learning journey. We're challenged by those with whom we differ, we get stumped by arguments we've not anticipated, and through it all we gain insight and experience. If we persevere, we come out with a better understanding of ourselves and the world around us.

If we instead bring some intellectual humility to the conversation—the same humility that serves us well by making discussions less combative—we might have a different experience altogether. It might open the door to serious conversation about serious problems that doesn't feel grave.

So, please, have some fun with it. Be open and honest. Be curious. Challenge yourselves as you challenge each other. Be humble—it doesn't make your ideas less valid. Enjoy every learning adventure that a thoughtful, constructive political conversation can bring.

By offering something that is instead positive and empowering, we can welcome a wider audience, not only of those who feel the need to take part, but also of so many who would now *want* to take part. Perhaps, it might reach, engage, and uplift someone close to you.

The Power of One

If you could empower one person in your life to have a healthier relationship with politics, who would it be? A colleague you find it awkward to work with? An old friend you've fallen out of touch with? An aunt or uncle? A daughter or son?

There is, of course, no wrong answer. All too many of us have relationships that have been soured by politics and our inability to discuss them in a healthy manner. Once you've built up a healthier political mindset, however—and please first make sure that you have—then one of the greatest things you can do is to share it in the interest of building or rebuilding a valuable relationship. To do so successfully, even once, can be life-changing.

This isn't a matter of the person you're reaching out to reaching out in turn to someone else, who reaches out to someone else, and so forth. That's not ultimately an efficient method of spreading the word or healing communities at a larger scale—if that's what you're going for, it's easier to just recommend this book (which I would appreciate, by the way).

Rather, the value of supporting healthy relationships through a healthier understanding of politics lies in those relationships themselves. Consider the difference that those close to you have made in your life. Consider every time you've felt the need to have someone to turn to, or been glad you've had someone to turn to. Especially in a time of ever-growing social isolation, where these relationships are fewer, having one more can make a profound difference.

Likewise, the potential to heal even one relationship in this way is a tremendous part of what makes my work, and the work of others in this space, worthwhile. Maybe, the prospect of changing just one life can provide some valuable motivation on your journey of building a healthier political mindset, too.

Of course, it's also perfectly reasonable to dream bigger.

---

1. "Nearing Holiday Season, Americans Weigh Family Estrangement - Harris Poll." Harris Poll, 3 Jan. 2025

2. Dunn, Amina. "Few Trump or Biden Supporters Have Close Friends Who Back the Opposing Candidate." Pew Research

3. Bay, NBC. "New Survey Reveals That Politics May Impact Romantic Relationships." NBC Bay Area, 20 Jan

Intermission

About the Author (Sort of)

Shortly after my fifth birthday, I lost my father to a brief and unexpected battle with cancer. I was too young at the time to fully understand what was happening, and my world was already changing so fast that the shock didn't hit me as it might have if it had happened years later. I *was* very much aware, however, of the way my family was affected, and it was seeing their response and the sadness they carried that would become one of the formative experiences of my life and my character.

To this day, my greatest fear is to be looked upon with a sense of disappointment, to invoke the thought of what might have been *if only*. This fear has since morphed into something of an ego-obsession with leaving a legacy, with bringing happiness to those around me and making a positive impact that can endure regardless of what comes of me (because of course, you never know). It is my most operative driving force in life decisions, a compass that at times has steered me toward impatience and impulse, that has required some work to balance with life's more practical needs and considerations.

As a youth, I was enamored with puzzles and games, problem-solving challenges in chess and math and even poetry—I liked trying to find those rhymes, and in another life, I might have gone on to become a rapper (I'd have been terrible). As I grew into adulthood, however, I began to sense a creeping lack of fulfillment. Although I was trying to apply my skills in the workforce, I didn't feel that I was making the impact, or bringing the positivity to others I knew I was capable of.

That changed in 2018, when I made my first major foray into politics, attempting to gather up enough steam to make an independent bid for Congress. I saw a need for dynamism in policymaking, for new and interesting ideas, and for a message that could unify. For the first time in my life, I was able to apply my love for problem-solving and my curiosity about the world around me into something that could somehow possibly make that world better. I felt a sense of purpose and direction. It was exciting.

I didn't go very far that year, and ultimately, I abandoned my pursuit before it became too costly, managing to return all the early donations I had received. I was not a credible candidate, neither experienced enough in public service nor refined enough in presentation. I lacked infrastructure and support, and I had underestimated some of the political winds I was up against. Even with all of this in mind, though, there was a frustrating sense that our politics, and the way we thought about politics, wasn't conducive to welcoming new voices or new ideas at all.

I still carry some of the policy notions I ran on—things like refocusing primary education to better inspire curiosity, or utilizing service programs to drive investment in a post-automation economy. I hope to talk about them in more depth, but the place for that is not here and the time for that is not now. I share this so you can understand, that a tremendous part of what drives my work in trying to foster a better conversation is that I want so dearly to be *in* that conversation.

I don't know how much of my story will resonate, but I do know I'm not the only one. Too many out there—some, I'm sure, with better and bigger ideas than my own—are not getting their chance to share their voice. I want them to be able to dream like I do. I want them to realize those dreams.

Above all, in the face of a broken discourse, one which stifles expression and breeds division and leads us to failing policy after failing policy, I refuse to stand idly by and watch. And so should you.

PART V

Yielding the Crop

YOUR GOAL: Think Big

What is the point of all this? Why have we spent all this time thinking about how to have better conversations with one another? What does it matter if our elected leadership continues to be mired in dysfunction, if our crises continue to worsen, and the state of our nation deteriorates while we stand by and watch?

It may well be that all of this would be worthwhile anyway, for giving you ways to improve your ability to process the world around you, to understand and communicate with different perspectives, and to maintain your mental health through it all. And who knows? Maybe it's not all so bad in the end, and things will calm down somehow.

Here's the thing, though—the state of our electoral politics is not inevitable. For all of the destructive cycles and incentives in play, there are ways to push back. For all of the faults in our current systems, we do still live in a democratic society. We have a say. We can change things.

Here's the other thing—the demand is there for unifiers and problem solvers. The demand is palpable for something different in our politics, some sort of alternative to the same old tired partisan brands. The people want leaders who exemplify the very virtues—thoughtfulness, transparency, honesty, creativity, a willingness to listen and learn—so essential to better discourse.

This book is not called *Better Political Conversational Techniques*. First of all, that would be a terrible title. And second, it wouldn't do justice to the scope of what I am attempting to cover. This is not solely about how we handle ourselves in interpersonal dialogue, or how we

as individuals think about politics. It's also about the upstream political drivers that have led us to this state of deep division, **and the
downstream political impact we can have with the right tools and
mindset.**

In the chapters ahead, we'll be going over the paths to political power, and how we can think practically and realistically about ways to alter
the electoral landscape. We'll be talking about what a movement toward
better politics may look like, and what overarching goals and vision it
should embrace. Finally, we'll be looking at the unique opportunities
of the modern day, and why it may not be so unreasonable to believe
that something that upholds the virtues of constructive discourse could
actually succeed in the political arena.

As with the first portion of this book, there will be cycles featured
and highlighted. As we move through understanding the tools and strat-
agems available to support political change, we'll also be looking at how
some of our previous destructive cycles can break, and how new, more
positive trends can begin to gain their own momentum.

Ultimately, it is the success of our voices and those we empower,
through the ideas we produce and through our ability to capitalize upon
the critical opportunities and needs of our day, that we can showcase the
bounty of what can be harvested upon common ground.

My goal is not for you to come away from this book a dreamer,
thinking how amazing it would be if only some miracle might happen.
I want you to come away *knowing* that making a political impact is
possible, and that you can play a part in positive change in the years
ahead.

13

Making It Political

And Being Realistic Along the Way

I n early 2025, the approval rating for the U.S. Congress went suddenly to 29%.[1] To be clear, it did not suddenly *fall* to 29%—in fact, it rose sharply, as it often does early in a new term. When it isn't enjoying such a crest, this number has tended in recent years around the late teens, plummeting as low as 9% in the early 2010s.

Despite this, members of our national legislature enjoy some remarkable job security. In 2022, roughly 94% of U.S. Representatives seeking reelection were successful in finding it, while every single sitting senator who ran won their race.[2] Those levels of incumbent success have become par for the course in recent decades, with the House rate climbing as high as 98% in 2004, while the Senate has averaged 88% incumbent success since 1990.

This juxtaposition, of a profoundly unpopular institution that appears so resistant to popular demand, is enough to make one lose hope in our political process. Indeed, quite a number have, writing off our elected government's lack of responsiveness and growing corruption as an ultimate inevitability, a foregone conclusion.

One could quite easily extend this pessimism, in fact, to dismiss efforts like mine. What point is there to have civil discourse among a few commoners, when those in real power are going to carry on all the same? If they're going to continue being divisive, performative, and ineffective in their public service?

Now, I wish I could offer some grand formula to fix it all, a surefire way to ensure that dynamic, pragmatic, and thoughtful problem-solvers can unseat the tired politicians of yesterday. Of course, it's not so simple, but we can start by examining the potential pathways to improvement.

Along my journey in the space of independent politics, third-party politics, and electoral reform, I will admit freely that I have not been a part of many won races. I have, however, learned a tremendous amount along my way, and I have seen a few standout candidates, with bridge-building mindsets and well-managed campaigns, come closer and closer than ever in recent memory.

To say that it is not possible to turn the tides of our elected politics is self-defeating—it discourages some of the best would-be public servants from ever vying for public office, while those who do are left to struggle with cynics quick to write them off. Moreover, those write-offs aren't wholly warranted, not only because of some broad notion that anything is possible and things might change, but because the realities of the situation are far less clear-cut than we tend to perceive.

To understand the practical considerations and challenges facing those who run is to begin to understand the bigger picture, and what hope we have to improve it. I'll be presenting the former group throughout the chapter. I'll also be doing so in the second person, to help you empathize with anyone looking to be the political change we need, and also, well, just in case you might be open to considering it.

If you have thought about running, or if you know anyone who might consider running for any level of office, I commend you. You have a real opportunity in front of you to change politics for the better.

Before you do that, though, there are a few things you should know.

Paths to Power

What does it take to run for office? Well, as one might imagine, the answer depends quite a bit on what office you're looking to run for. Campaigns for Senator are going to have starkly different requirements and dynamics from bids for Town Council, and even two races for the same level of office can offer wildly different running experiences depending on the area, the election rules in play, and who else might be interested in the seat.

Likely the cleanest way to break down different positions of political power is by their level, and here, we have a few well-defined categories. Elections for federal office are administered by the federal government and subject to national rules and processes for offices like U.S. Senator, U.S. Representative, and U.S. President. At the state level, elections are run by the state, most prominently for the governorship and state legislative bodies. The county offices are often commissioner roles whose elections are overseen by the county (notice the pattern here), and then we have a range of municipal offices run by cities and towns, as well as school board offices, often with their own districts and dynamics.

The top of this list, as one might imagine, is where the barrier to entry tends to be highest, and where much of the national attention focuses. Candidates for House and Senate are expected to routinely raise millions of dollars to maintain competitive races, while the race for the presidency tends to draw huge attention and scrutiny, along with billions of dollars spent on campaigns. Before all of those more visible elements come into play, however, candidates for these offices often are required to raise significant amounts of money and collect thousands of signatures to even appear on the ballot.

You would not be wrong to think that this would be quite the undertaking for an upstart, but you *would* be mistaken if you concluded that running for a lower office should be an easy affair in comparison. No, even beyond the gubernatorial races—which regularly garner national attention and feature campaign spends in the millions—any credible bid for state or county office demands a months-long team effort to appeal to thousands upon thousands of voters, with very real and impactful policymaking power on the line. Unlike with federal offices, however, these races also need to contend with significant down-ballot pressure, where lower-information voters focused on more big-name electoral goings-on may vote along their party lines and have a profound effect on results, making it especially hard for anyone to run as a difference maker outside the two-party paradigm.

If you want to avoid these busy ballots, you may be better served running for a local office, where elections often happen in off-years. These races are also frequently non-partisan, with less influence from state- and county-level political machines (though they may still wield significant influence), and generally more focus on direct interaction with prospective voters.

With that said, being able to compete for an office more realistically should never be reason enough to run. Any seat of power is going to have an important role with important decision-making responsibilities, and understanding the nature and scope of the role at hand is essential to being taken seriously at any level. To treat a bid as some sort of stepping stone or statement is to disrespect it, and prospective voters, donors, and supporters would be able to tell.

If you're running to become a problem-solver and change things, then you can continue assessing the path forward by understanding *where* you plan to be running. Again, this is not something the vast majority of potential candidates have a choice in, but it is an important factor to consider. Where you run may affect the rules for eligibility, the process of filing your candidacy, the timings and deadlines involved, the limitations on fundraising, and the partisan or non-partisan nature of the race.

Typically, one qualifies for ballot access by gathering signatures or raising a requisite quantity of funds, and often by doing both. State, county, and national parties can help tremendously in these processes, and that's also another way in which they exercise power, selection, and control over who ascends the ranks.

The Trouble with Gerald[3]

Of course, where you run also profoundly affects the makeup of your voters, and the competitive dynamics of the race as a result. Districts can be wildly lopsided toward Republicans or Democrats, or incredibly tight. Some may have a large number of independent voters, while others contain relatively few. And then there are the local demographics, which can be deeply intertwined with voter values, priorities, and tendencies.

One of the challenges in understanding district dynamics—and indeed, one of the major obstacles to posing any legitimate challenge as an outsider—is the fact that many of these districts are profoundly unnatural. They are drawn and divided primarily by partisan commissions in ways that are favorable to majority parties in charge and incumbent officials, a practice we know as gerrymandering. For all the earlier talk about rigged and broken games, this throws many contests squarely into the former camp—it is, frankly, a legal ability to rig that comes with seated power.

> To understand the practical considerations and challenges that face those running is to begin to understand the greater political picture and what hope we have to improve it.

As with any other obstacle, however, the problem of gerrymandering should not make us abandon all hope, but it should be accounted for properly. If you are making a bid as part of a minority party, be aware of the gaps in voter registration you face. If you are thinking of what to run for or what campaign to support, also keep in mind that your district will vary depending on what you decide—for example, your State Senate district may be more competitive than your State House district, which may be more competitive than your U.S. House district, while your statewide races aren't going to be affected by gerrymandering at all, but might be wildly uncompetitive regardless.

The most lopsided districts, whether borne of gerrymandering or not, also create an interesting opportunity for independents running, as they may only face competition from a single major party, and may be able to avoid spoiler stigma as a result. During my time at Forward, I referred to these situations as flanking opportunities, where it was possible to build a coalition of underrepresented minority party voters, unaffiliated voters, and even majority party members dissatisfied with what the primaries were producing, thereby gaining a potential edge in numbers.

Indeed, these are the scenarios where non-major party challengers have been most successful at the federal level in recent years, with independent senatorial efforts by Evan McMullin (in Utah in 2022) and Dan Osborn (in Nebraska in 2024) claiming well over 40% of the final tally against sole Republican opponents. These offer a valuable potential stratagem, and we'll be taking a closer look in a bit.

Further complicating matters are variations in rules and election structures. Simple plurality voting remains predominant, but Ranked-choice voting has made some traction in recent decades, creating new competitive dynamics—particularly for races of three or more—in a few areas. Meanwhile, state variations in open vs. closed primaries (that is, those that allow for independent voters to participate or not) profoundly change the incentives and dynamics of the primary stage, and even the number of voters registering as independent or unaffiliated.

One of the most significant variables in how you'll have to approach a campaign, however, is whether you will be running in a primary at all. In some races, this stage is more decisive and impactful than the general, while in others, you may be put in the position of having to run two distinct campaigns appealing to rather different audiences.

Closed primaries, in particular, have dramatically different dynamics from their general election counterparts. Featuring turnout percentages that can fall into the teens in non-presidential years,[4] they tend to be decided by a relatively small group of party base partisans, who are more politically energized and more riled up than most every other segment of the voting populace. The accompanying reality is that these primaries are the most susceptible to partisan pandering, and by extension, the more exploitative behaviors of various PACs and special interests.

If you're running as an independent, you can avoid this portion of the elective process. Of course, you'll also be foregoing state party support, and you may be subject to specific ballot access restrictions and requirements. Once you're through all of that, you'll need to contend with the commonly held perception that independents almost never win, and the idea that they're more often acting as election spoilers.

As a reminder, **you don't need to be an independent to be a bridge-builder or an ambassador for better discourse.** How you present these things, however, may vary considerably depending on what audience you're speaking to and what you're running for. If you want to be an executive—say, a mayor or a governor—you may have a unique opportunity to help facilitate and mediate deliberative processes. If you're looking to become a legislator, then you understand the composition of the legislature, whether it's tightly divided or wildly lopsided, and how you could viably drive it toward more productivity and effectiveness.

All of this messaging may play differently depending on the demographics and priorities of the voting populace you're dealing with. A general election will feature a broad range of constituents (including many not in your party) who want to ensure their voices are heard and represented, and you will need to make this case. If you're working your way through a partisan primary against more fiery and uncompromising opponents, meanwhile, it may help to position yourself as an effective messenger of your party's particular values.

Whatever pathways may be available to you, it's also going to help profoundly to put yourself in the shoes of the voter, and to do your best to understand what you're offering when you ask for their support, and what it is they're hearing when they hear you speak—because it may not always be what you're trying to say.

Walking the Walk

It's time once again to take a step back and consider the perspectives of others. When we talk about bringing a better kind of politics to the electoral arena, we might have in mind a whole range of nice things we want to do and behaviors we want to exemplify once elected. It's one thing to imagine and to promise, though, and another altogether to get voters to buy in.

The tenets of better discourse sound dandy coming from a politician or a candidate. The trouble is, politicians promise lots of wonderful things. To put it mildly, they do not always deliver, and understandably, most voters have adjusted their expectations.

Saying you're going to do X, Y, and Z doesn't mean, in the eyes of the common voter, that you're going to do it. Having patient, deep, one-to-one transformative conversations isn't remotely scalable when you're dealing with thousands of voters. Exemplifying the principles at hand, however, such as valuing conversation, engaging with different perspectives, and working to make others feel heard, can make a difference, and it is possible to do so through a range of practices.

In this case, the most direct way to practice what you preach is often through town halls and direct voter engagement events. How you listen, how you handle arguments and emotions, and how you navigate conversations can all go a long way in helping people understand the kind of public servant you intend to be. And beyond the standard town hall, there also exist a number of newer, innovative approaches to facilitating group conversations and healthy civic deliberations. Utilizing these not only shows that you're committed to making people feel heard, but that you're willing to put the work in to make it happen.

Outside these events, it's essential to maintain a tone conducive to problem-solving in any messages that face the public, and not just those about what kind of leader you are. When writing press releases, filling out website copy, or posting on social media, it is exceedingly easy to fall into divisive language and tactics when talking about critical issues and the failures of incumbents or their parties. If you want to stand out from the noise, it's going to be important not to fall into these and their promise of short-term gains.

Likewise, the tone and tenor of a faithful public servant and a committed problem-solver should be maintained when speaking in front of the public. This includes interviews, podcast and media appearances, and debates. These are going to be challenging environments, so whatever standard you want to claim about the kind of civility and positivity you hold to, make sure it is a standard you're going to be able to sustain.

You may encounter hecklers and naysayers and skeptics ready to press as hard as they can. You *will* encounter opponents operating under starkly different incentives than your friendlier partners in conversation. Some adjustment will be required.

You will need patience and a thick skin. You will also need to have a healthy support system at home, through your friends and your loved ones, those who you know will be there when things are hard. This, more so than any other prerequisite for a foray into politics, is something you do not want to underestimate the importance of.

All of this is just what is demanded of you internally. Aside from those pieces, you'll also need to build up the resources, infrastructure, and public support necessary to run a successful campaign, if you want to have a real shot at winning.

Hey now, I never said this was going to be easy.

The $16 Billion Dollar Question

Now we come to one of the elephants in the room: the looming, sometimes overwhelming presence of money in politics.

The 2024 federal election cycle saw some $15.9 billion in total spend.[5] While the 2020 cycle was comparable, the overall trend has been increasingly toward larger dollar amounts. Somewhere around $6 billion—less than half of these recent totals—was spent in the presidential years of 2012 and 2016. Going back to the 2000 presidential election, the spend again halves to $3 billion. Back in 1992, before Gingrich's revolution broke fundraising barriers, the entire federal cycle barely cracked the one billion dollar mark—still no small amount, but a far cry from just a few decades later, even adjusting for inflation.

Just as it was with the incumbency rates, it's easy to have a bleak outlook here, about what happens to genuine public servants who don't intend to cater to powerful special interests and influential PACs. But these numbers, while intimidating, may not tell the complete story.

At the federal level, roughly 90% of candidates who outspend their opponents wind up winning their races.[6] This number might seem high, but it becomes dramatically less impressive when you factor in the number of lopsided races and barely-challenged incumbents factoring into the data. Adjust further for a bit of statistical confounding—that is, the perceived winner drawing more donations and interest because of their perceived status, rather than gaining the status because of their superior fundraising—and you see a correlation that is still clear but far from decisive. The bigger spend will often win, but it's not a foregone conclusion—at least, not until we start believing that it is.

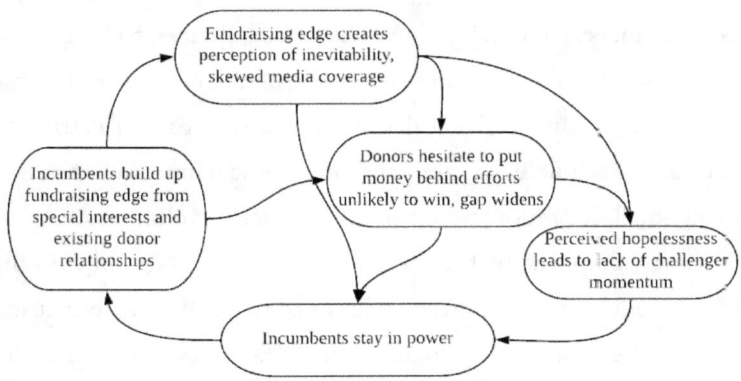

There are several recent trends and developments that may make leaner runs more feasible. New media, such as podcasts and Substacks, combine with social media to create more avenues for free promotion and messaging. Sophisticated voter data analysis tools (sophisticated tools, that is—not tools to analyze sophisticated voters) are more readily available at relatively lower cost. AI has made elements of creating copy and otherwise presenting a professional appearance easier and more affordable.

But that's not the end of the story, either. Sure, running lean can be a potential boon to challengers without the backing of political machines or huge special interests, but how lean can one run and still contend? To figure that out, we need to consider where all that money is ultimately going.

The classic image of campaign spending is buying a big, fancy advertising spot to broadcast a message. Indeed, these are major expenditures that account for quite a chunk of spending in big-ticket campaigns, but they're also far less of a factor beyond federal races, and even when they do come into play, the jury is still out on how effective they are.[7]

At lower levels of office, one of the largest slices of the spending pie belongs to mailers and printed materials (federal races, to be clear, do utilize these as well). Not only is this one of the main tools for mass communication on smaller scales, it's also a vital part of getting the fundraising machine in motion, and one of the main mechanisms for drawing small-dollar donations and even attracting volunteers.

Those volunteers, by the way, aren't really free. Not only do they need to be adequately resourced and trained to be effective, but at scale they need the oversight of qualified field managers—and those field managers don't work cheap (nor should they).

Another important expenditure that is often overlooked is CRM—that's Customer Relationship Management—and data. Running any kind of "smart" campaign demands the ability to make critical insights, but detailed voter information is often cost-intensive, and just being able to keep track of it all often requires a team of working professionals.

It's worth noting that the sort of candidates who have been most successful in finding outsize success without traditional mainstream channels of support aren't always the mediating type. Both in terms of capitalizing on social media energy for free publicity, and in terms of garnering small-dollar support without relying on special interests, it is those populist firebrands that tend to be the best positioned to take advantage of these alternative avenues.

Now, bringing populist energy and being a bridge-builder aren't mutually exclusive things. The conundrum remains, however, whether a candidate can embrace civility, intellectual humility, and integrity as a public servant, and actually *gain* from doing so. In fact, the question may well remain whether one can do so without severely impeding their ability to compete and win.

Do you have to win to be successful? Not necessarily. There's no law that says that you have to be trying to win, and plenty of candidates outside the mainstream do run to make a statement. But when the most positive candidates with the most interesting ideas are relegated to losing effort after losing effort, it is naturally going to be disheartening to anyone hoping for our societal outcomes to improve.

Breaking the Viability Loop

Approval ratings for our elected leaders are abysmally low. Faith in our institutions is low. Confidence in our democracy, and the direction it's going, is beyond wavering. And yet, the people know all this—at least those who follow this sort of thing do—and the more that they see things failing to change despite it, the more resigned they become to the notion that they never will.

If you should desire to run and to bring a better voice to our politics—your voice—and to bring the mindsets and principles of better discourse, you will not be met with immediate vitriol. If you handle your interactions well and have a positive reputation in your district, you will see far more smiles than frowns on your trail. You will, however, be met with one crucial, often unspoken, question—*what hope do you have?*

The answer cannot be simply that you believe in yourself, that things will be different this time than in every similar effort to date. It cannot be that you're simply *so* virtuous and principled that the voters are bound to see the light (also, please don't use phrases like this). There needs to be something tangible, a real reason to believe that you can succeed where others have faltered.

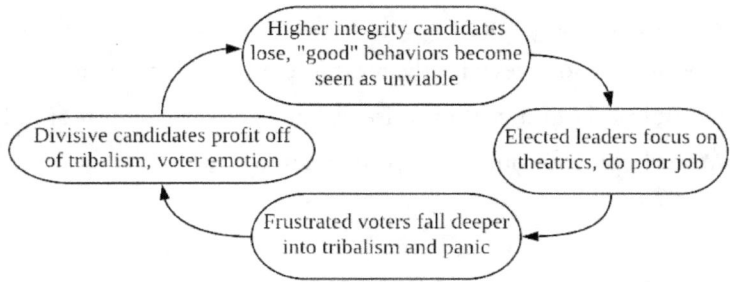

I'm reminded again of a friend of mine, who commented that he would most certainly pay his workers a generous wage if he were only a CEO. As I told him, it's great that he would, but when doing the right thing is going to put you at some disadvantage, it's easy to understand why the trends are pointing the other way.

It's the same idea here. **If being civil is a hindrance to office-seekers, even if it's something that they can overcome with enough name recognition and connections, it's not going to scale.** Being the "real deal" has to offer some tangible, strategic benefit in order for our political ecosystem to start selecting for it.

And it absolutely can! Lest we forget, there is tremendous demand for something new and better, and this would certainly qualify. The number of people rejecting and tuning out from our system offers another indicator of yearning for an alternative, and a huge unclaimed pool of supporters and voters to tap into. And as crises worsen, there's a growing need for real solutions, offering a boon to anyone with new, dynamic, and promising ideas.

Of course, a breakthrough win by a high-quality candidate could change it all, demanding attention while seriously shifting perceptions. One marquee upset can be the model for upstart candidates in its vein, and voters given real reason to believe might be far easier to activate and energize.

But therein may lie the real key: that all of these efforts to bring better politics to elected office are inherently intertwined, and that real success may come from figuring out how we—the ones trying to champion collaboration—can ourselves work together.

---

1. Gallup. "Congress and the Public." Gallup.com, Gallup, 2024

2. "Incumbent Politicians Enjoy Record Reelection in an Aging Congress." OpenSecrets News, 12 Oct. 2023

3. Gerrymandering, it should be noted, takes its name from Elbridge Gerry, the eventual fifth Vice President of the United States, who pioneered the practice while running for Massachusetts governor in the early 1810's. Gerald, whoever Gerald is, is innocent.

4. Ferrer, Joshua, and Michael Thorning. "2022 Primary Turnout | Bipartisan Policy Center." Bipartisanpolicy.org, 6 Mar. 2023

5. Bryner, Sarah, and Brendan Glavin. "Total 2024 Election Spending Projected to Exceed Previous Record - OpenSecrets News." OpenSecrets News, 8 Oct. 2024

6. "Did Money Win?" OpenSecrets, 2022

7. Kwok, Roberta . "How Much Do Campaign Ads Matter?" Kellogg Insight, 1 Nov. 2021

14

What Future Are We Trying to Build?
And What if We Don't Agree?

One individual running to change democracy, or in pursuit of whatever noble goal, may not always be able to inspire real voter excitement. There's only so much that a single official can do, after all—especially in a legislative context—and even in the best case, they might seem like an outlier, a drop in the ocean of unsavory politics, doomed to swim against the current until the whirlpool takes them, too.

A movement, on the other hand, is a different story. A movement can create new voting blocs, push new ideas to the fore, and seriously shift electoral competitive dynamics. In their pursuit of doing so, such endeavors often provide member candidates with valuable tools and resources, as well as with the strength of a greater brand.

These movements may take the form of a PAC (Political Action Committee), a new party, a nonprofit, or even a loosely organized collective. From the Whigs to Lincoln's GOP, to more recent factions in the Justice Democrats and Tea Party Republicans, these group efforts have shown themselves plenty capable as change-makers within the political arena.

Now, when a new group emerges, people are naturally going to have questions: What does this group stand for? Who's behind it? What are its intentions? When operating in the space of new politics that defy how we think about and approach the civic problems of our time, these are not always going to be easy questions to answer—but answering them well is critically important.

At this point, some would expect me to tie everything together and declare that a healthy, civil discourse should itself be the North Star to the next great movement, the guiding light toward which a generation of high-minded candidates will lead. They would be wrong.

I have been a part of more than one effort that defined itself along these more philosophical lines. I have seen, more than once, the voter confusion and apprehension to which it leads. The trouble is, this sort of guiding philosophy is a style and ethos of governance, and groups looking to empower candidates along such lines are asking essentially for the means to power without a clear end in mind.

When you ask for power without giving some picture of the policy outcomes, it is quite natural for people to conclude one of two things: either that you haven't thought things all the way through, or that you have a hidden agenda, a vision that you're not sharing. Neither one of these conclusions is favorable.

What is needed is a vision, an idea of what kind of changes, what kind of society, these candidates and this organization can drive toward. It needs to be dynamic and exciting, without seeming fanciful or unrealistic, clear and understandable without being obvious or generic. And in creating this vision, any aspiring organization must contend with the tension between empowering the individual voices of candidates and voters, and defining the goals and intentions of the organization itself.

It is by no means an easy task. Making it work, however, may mean the difference between breaking through the barriers of our political system, and ultimately faltering in that pursuit.

What Do We Mean, 'We People?'

Understanding the collective vision of any organizational effort requires first understanding what the collective is. Who, exactly, is coming together? Why?

It would be fair to say that I am calling here for some kind of movement, but of whom? I'm writing, after all, to both liberals and conservatives alike, to the politically entrenched as well as the politically homeless. What exactly would such a broad group unify around, other than some general principles of good conversation—principles which, as I've already contended, aren't enough for a compelling vision?

The thing is, the movement toward a better politics doesn't have to be a singular organizational effort at all. There could be a Republican faction, a collective of Democrats, and a band of independents all operating at once, each in some way exemplifying a unifying mindset and embracing a constructive discourse. There could be minor parties, nonprofits, PACs, and more serving in complementary functions, whether these organizations formally collaborate with each other or not.

Within this paradigm, there is far more room to have a well-defined set of values and vision. If we have a shared understanding of the greater conversation of which we are a part, it allows us to fit more clearly into our roles within that conversation—what we're advocating for, what perspectives we're representing, and what potential excesses and inefficiencies we are most closely guarding against.

Through segmentation, it is easier for each organization to have a range of stated goals and priorities while appealing to a wider audience and adhering to some common principles. Moreover, thought leaders within each group can be more in tune with their respective organizations' core values and sensibilities. Eventually, when some brand and trust are established, these groups may, in cases, merge together to form broader and more powerful entities. Early on, however, there is no such need for a singular umbrella.

Along this pathway, the first steps are for leaders and founders to build out their groups' messaging and core infrastructure. Once this is in place—and in many places it already is—the next challenge becomes attracting quality candidates. This part, as one might imagine, is also quite important.

The Box Problem

Among those I've encountered who seem most apt to take political action, there seems to be something of a defining throughline—a dissatisfaction with the way our politics is presented, and in particular with the way that our society so often reduces us to simple labels. It is a free-thinking and open-minded spirit, and it leads us to a little conundrum I like to call the Box Problem.

The problem is this: **You're not going to inspire a movement of outside-the-box thinkers to coalesce by simply offering a new box.** Regardless of the specifics, any top-down, prescriptive policy set is bound to encounter resistance. Where the individual expression and unique voices of candidates are your most vital assets, it makes little sense to risk stifling them. Open-mindedness and intellectual humility are such defining elements of better discourse, and they would be undermined by a rigid and dogmatic approach.

A large number of minor party efforts have been of this small box variety. Greens, Libertarians, and others have not significantly innovated upon the major party approach to defining ideology and policy, or to disseminating these through their membership. They tend, as a result, to have niche appeal, and fail repeatedly to capture not only a broader swath of high-quality candidates, but also the great majority of voters dissatisfied with our two biggest options. It is not only a method unlikely to win elections—to that end, these efforts can still succeed in calling attention to some particular issue or idea, which is what they primarily seek to do anyway—it distorts our perception of what is and is not viable within the political realm, giving undue credence to the notion that third parties can never win.

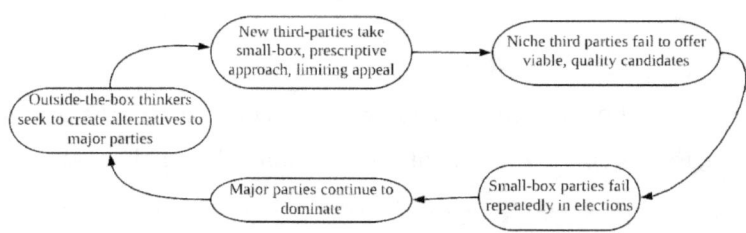

Far more success has been found in non-duopoly efforts built around individual flag-bearers. Ross Perot earned nearly 20% of the popular vote in the 1992 Presidential Election, while more recently, Robert F. Kennedy, Jr. managed to draw significant national attention (and eventually pivot into a cabinet position) through his 2024 run. This approach, however, does not scale well, and relies heavily on singular leaders with enormous monetary and media resources. Moreover, these efforts tend to focus on the elections where the fear of spoilers runs highest.

When it comes to creating wider and more durable movements, there is a tension that needs to be wrestled with, between the ethos of approaching politics with an open mind—and the sense of empowerment that that offers to candidates and voters—and the need for a compelling and clear vision. It's not a reason to give up on the exercise altogether, but it is something to be aware of—as I and others have learned the hard way.

To address this tension, one may attempt to temper how prescriptive and clear-cut policy stances are. By doing so, a party or PAC can indicate an intellectually humble and pluralistic approach, embracing the ethos that more voices can help guide toward the best solutions. On a practical level, however, this is a difficult balance to strike. Finding the proper language, without coming across as vague or noncommittal to the lay voter, is a daunting task.

Another approach is to message by example, pointing to specific ideas from individual candidates as models of what the organization can bring, rather than rigid standards of what it must be in every case. Ironically, taking this route also leads us to a box of sorts, but it should be a more welcome one to see.

Wielding the Toolbox

Of the many complaints I've heard leveled against our status quo, one of the most interesting has dealt with the monotony of partisan talking points. Many of the key issues for mainstream Democrats and Republicans—taxes and government programs, guns, abortion, and so on—are well-trodden territory, and the solutions and rallying cries have changed little in the past fifty years. For new movements, embracing the innovative breadth of a toolbox not only capitalizes on a market need for new ideas, but it does so in style.

The toolbox doesn't just leave room for individual voices to shine and for individual candidates to feel empowered. It actively shines a light upon them, pushing them forward as exemplars. From an organizational messaging standpoint, it helps to illustrate the potential benefit of empowered and motivated public servants. At the same time, it's also something of an ego boost for these exemplary candidates—and when you're asking people to embark on the journey of running for office, this sort of thing can come in handy.

The elements of such a toolbox don't have to be fully fleshed-out policy proposals. They can be pieces of potential solutions, such as a particular tax incentive or a new sort of government program. They can even be approaches to discussing issues or engaging with communities. Any one of these things can showcase the range of dynamic thinking within a movement, and the way that it can vary based on local context.

It's not only candidates who can be empowered. The idea that one size does not fit all, that each champion has the freedom to bring their own variations and innovations to the table, also signals to voters that their local sensibilities will be considered, and that their unique voices will be heard.

At its best, utilizing the toolbox is not just a way to create effective messaging while maintaining an ethos of open-mindedness and intellectual humility. It is a way to turn these virtues into advantages, to paint a picture of a political future that is *only* possible when such principles are embraced.

Forging a Fulcrum

But wait a minute, one might ask, how much of a difference can a handful of noble-minded candidates really make? Aren't our halls of legislature cluttered, regardless, with the politics of division? How many cycles would it take to purge all that?

The thing is, a tertiary political movement, especially one trying to create some kind of mediation between the partisan establishments, isn't beholden to the same incentives that the major parties are. Because those major parties are still going to be there in the foreseeable term, all it takes to fundamentally change our incentives is to consistently deny either a legislative majority. This buffer, which needs not be more than a handful of elected officials, can create what is known as a *fulcrum* within the political apparatus, a vital balance within the system.

The onus of building such a thing does not fall solely on independents or third parties. Democrats and Republicans committed to a better discourse and a more effective process can also choose to break from their respective establishments and help forge a coalition. Although their own incentives and pressures from party leadership need to first be carefully considered, those who are able to work toward creating this balancing force can go a long way toward empowering their parties to become the best versions of themselves.

The presence of a fulcrum does a few things. When neither of the two dominant parties can claim a majority, neither can strong-arm and force through laws simply by keeping its members in line. In turn, the notion of the Other Side "taking power" loses a great deal of its fear-in-voking luster, limiting the would-be rabble rousers who might try to take advantage of it. Appealing beyond the party base becomes essential to legislate anything, and the incentives for a constructive and collaborative problem-solving process grow.

All this does not somehow eliminate or marginalize the partisans. On the contrary, it creates a situation where they are empowered to be advocates and ambassadors of their principles and brands, working to ensure that their ideologies and their constituents' voices are well represented in the broader conversation.

Without the pendulum swings of a zero-sum, two-party system, the possibility of long-term planning and lawmaking suddenly opens up in a way not seen in modern times. Consistency and stability allow for breakthroughs in infrastructure planning, for greater peace of mind in immigration and foreign policy, and even for a stock market less beholden to the speculative swings of each election season.

As things stand, both the U.S. House and the U.S. Senate are tightly divided bodies, with gaps in Republican and Democratic membership rarely exceeding ten percentage points. Within this paradigm, breaking through does not require outnumbering or overpowering either of these institutional megaliths. **Well-run campaigns by quality candidates capable of appealing to a range of audiences, in places where they can run free of spoiler stigma, can lead to all the wins needed.**

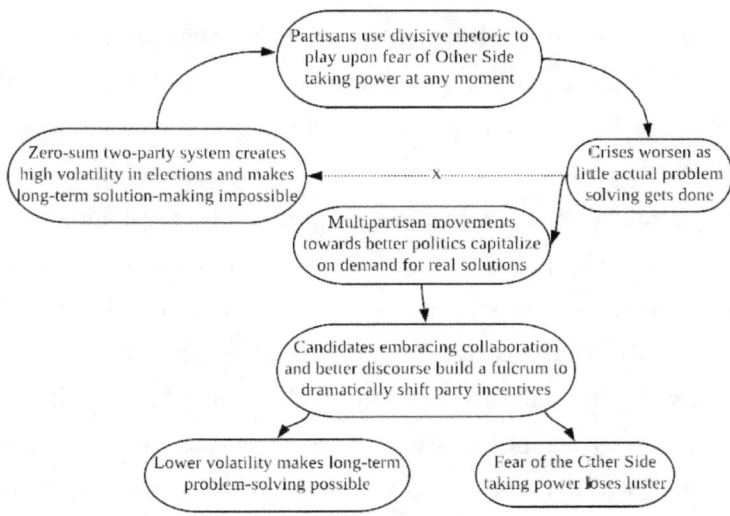

Over time, subterfuge from the party establishments can also help, further lowering the threshold to putting a fulcrum in place. More sitting politicians than you might imagine are problem solvers at heart, tied down by broken incentives in a broken system. And while they may certainly discourage us at times, we should not abandon hope, either in their ultimate integrity of these individuals or in the democracy that they are tasked to uphold.

Making the Global Case

It is not only for our own sake that we should strive for a healthy discourse and a more functional governance. **If we believe truly in the principles of our democratic society and in the freedoms of ex-**

pression that we uphold, then it behooves us not only to maintain these freedoms but to showcase the best that they can produce.

Our democracy is not something to be taken for granted. In the modern age of communications and technology, personal liberties are for many a scary notion. They can be not only abused by their holders, but by demagogues and forces of corruption, or by any ill-intentioned actor. At a certain point, they threaten to create an unsustainable and dangerous situation, where festering chaos leads to manipulation of the masses, which then worsens the chaos, intensifying the spiral.

Lowering the political temperature is vital. Understanding the complexity of the checks and balances we need to create, to address the abuses happening within ever-evolving power structures, is vital. Being able to communicate clearly, calmly, and effectively with one another, both personally and politically, is vital.

If we believe in the principles of our democratic society and in the freedoms of expression that we uphold, then it behooves us not only to maintain these freedoms, but to showcase the best that they can produce.

At our country's founding, the American experiment excited many in its embrace of liberty and Enlightenment thought. It brought about an era of upheaval and revolution by way of its imitators. Although not every movement that followed was successful, the shockwaves from our ideas rang loud and clear.

We remain a poster child for liberal structures and personal freedoms, for better or for worse. How we fare may determine whether the leaders and change-makers of tomorrow, from all around the world, should try to emulate the American experiment and the ideals of our nation, or whether they should be more drawn to the order and security promised by more authoritarian structures.

Whether our democracy works, in turn, may depend on what works within our democracy. It is incumbent upon us not only to embrace better discourse and a problem-solving mindset personally, but to strategically position this mindset and its ambassadors as best we can for success in the political arena. Their success is far from guaranteed, but there is no better time to try than now.

15

Why Now? (Reprise)

A Realist's Reasons Things Can Change

I have many a fond memory of growing up around Boston, but the taxi prices weren't one of them. The city is relatively small compared to its metro area, and the cabs were limited to picking up fares in the various towns to which they belonged. Riders, as a result, would often be saddled with the costs of lonely return trips, and the prices we paid compared unfavorably to our archrival, New York, and other big cities with wider city limits. It wasn't the end of the world, but I do recall sitting in the back seat more than once thinking something along the lines of, *"y'know, this seems dumb."*

What I was experiencing was a market inefficiency, and, lo and behold, it would be met with a market correction. Uber emerged at a price point starkly different from what locals were used to, and quickly established itself as a major disruptor in the area. Its growth in Boston was expedited by the local need for more affordable private transportation, and the company seized the opportunity. Generally speaking, that's how things in business are supposed to work.

This is not to deify Uber or other ridesharing businesses, which have certainly brought their own share of serious questions around regulation, fair competition, and the gig economy. It is worth noting, however, that incredible change is possible if we work to understand trends and problems, needs and demands, and opportunities for dynamic innovation and disruption. It's a manner of thinking taught in every business school around the world, but in the realm of politics, it feels often like a foreign concept.

Sure, we might be unhappy with our political reality, but a great many treat it as one would weather or fate. As our elected bodies become increasingly out-of-touch and ineffective in the face of abysmal approval and worsening crises, election after election, a sense of disempowerment builds upon itself. People, understandably, lose hope.

This sort of despondency is more than a shame. It's also every bit as susceptible to abuse as blind zealotry or sports-fanatic team loyalty. It's a massive bloc of voter apathy and inactivity that incumbents and party bosses can count on cycle after cycle—they know that some 30% of the more tuned-out eligible voters are going to stay home every general election, while over 80% are likely to skip the primary.[1] They don't worry about those folks, and why should they?

When a would-be alternative tries to emerge, it is this despondency that our political machines rely upon as the first line of defense, to reinforce the thinking that whatever new thing is there probably won't work, because nothing ever really changes anyway.

No, our politics is not going to improve simply because we want it to. But if we can move beyond the simplistic—and false—notion that there's nothing we can do about it, we can start to see some of the bigger picture, and the real inroads available to positive change.

What we may find is not only opportunity, but *growing* opportunity. By utilizing modern communication and technology, by tapping into the deep dissatisfaction with current leadership, and by appreciating properly the obstacles we face, we can drive toward better politics in a way that has not been possible before.

Political Industry, Political Opportunity

One of the most effective methods used by the political pow-ers-that-be to discourage challengers is by invoking the so-called spoiler effect—the notion that a vote for any kind of third option rather than the lesser of two evils risks handing the win to the greater evil. It's an idea that came to modern prominence after the 1992 Election, when Ross Perot's independent effort managed to snag some 20% of the popular vote in a relatively close race (of note, exit polls didn't seem to indicate that his voters would have skewed strongly one way or the other),[2] and was further ingrained into the public conscience after Ralph Nader's Green Party run in the nailbiter 2000 election. The idea capitalizes upon both a profound fear of the Other Side and a sense of defeatism that comes from seeing underdogs try and fail. It's a loud and clear message, that gains strength from every worsening crisis and unpopular presidency—each of which make the Other Side gaining power more frightful, and the perceived risk of voting any third option greater.

The fear of this spoiler effect is so overwhelming, in fact, that a signif-icant portion of the independent political space is dedicated to avoiding the obstacle altogether through electoral reforms. Indeed, proposals like ranked-choice voting—which would allow candidates for any given race to be voted for in order of preference—would render void some of the talking points around spoilers and wasted votes. Unfortunately, the barrier to instituting such reforms tends to be quite high, and the notion that nothing in politics will change until reforms are implemented—a statement I've heard verbatim more than once—is itself profoundly de-featist. It is a reductive assessment of the problem at hand, and dismisses the potential for success that non-duopoly candidates—and other challengers to the partisan status quo—already have.

Yes, the spoiler effect and the fear thereof are relevant to the Presidential Election and to other tightly contested races between a Republican and a Democrat. While this has become the common image of what an American election is, however, it is far from representative of most voting contests.

> Our politics is not going to improve just because we want it to. But if we can move beyond the simplistic notion that there is nothing we can do, we can start to see the bigger picture, and the real inroads available to positive change.

As I've alluded before, a great many races every cycle usually go uncontested—some 70%, in fact if local contests are counted—or otherwise uncompetitive. These create the best environments for non-duopoly challengers to build coalitions to outflank incumbents, as Evan McMullin and Dan Osborn modeled in their 2022 Utah and 2024 Nebraska bids for U.S. Senate, respectively. McMullin would finish with 43% of the vote in his race, while Osborn earned 47% in his own—both ran without a large national movement behind them, and still both far outperformed the major party challengers who preceded them.

This flanking approach isn't restricted to independents or minor party efforts, either. In the early 2000s, the Massachusetts Republican Party, led by gubernatorial candidate Mitt Romney and his eventual lieutenant, Kerry Healey, positioned itself as a necessary balance of power in the deep blue state. Their brand and style were markedly different from the national GOP, and their unique appeal proved successful, resulting in multiple successful gubernatorial bids in the years that followed, in a state where Republican candidates for President were and continue to be routinely blown out.

Each district and each race presents its own opportunities, from low-quality incumbents to overbearing parties-in-power without any proper checks. **Voters want choice, they want to be heard, and they want to have alternatives. All of these demands demand attention.** Some of the worst cases of corruption and decay in leadership come from political machines that lack real competition, with plenty of easy examples to point to—Democrats in California, New York, and Chicago; Republicans in Alabama, Mississippi, and so forth—on either side, to remind people of this fundamental notion that power needs limitations.

Modern opportunities for political change, however, go beyond demographics and approval rates. New media offers cost-effective publicity to dynamic thinkers, providing platforms for long-term conversation where they can go beyond the punchy one-liners favored by the old partisans. New technology, meanwhile, allows for advanced and accessible tools for campaign management, voter data analysis, and mass outreach, making financially leaner runs more possible than ever.

Decades into our current Culture Wars, a fatigue has set in for many, and those many may welcome messages of reason and understanding—IF those messages can break through the noise. In the face of a tired politics that produces underwhelming leadership and poor solutions, there is real opportunity for change-making movements—but success comes down to effective organizational strategy, as well as the strength of the individual candidates and ideas that these movements push forward.

Modern Solvers for Modern Problems

It is not some partisan myth that we are experiencing terrible crises, or that some of these crises are seriously worsening. For all the natural impulse to panic and yell louder in the face of trouble, however, it is in fact this seriousness, depth, and complexity in our issues that most necessitates a thoughtful approach. It is not despite the trouble that we should work to create an analytical, collaborative, and healthy discourse, but because of it. **A productive problem-solving process, after all, is the only way to solve hard problems.**

Earlier, I shared a story of a woman running for the office of State Representative in Florida, whose campaign I was helping to support. She wanted to bring more attention to the state's spiraling costs of home insurance, but was told by a strategist that the issue was "unsexy." Nonetheless, she kept it as a hallmark of her campaign.

This was an independent candidate facing a mountain of obstacles—eventually, she would lose largely to down-ballot pressure. Before she did, however, she drew a tremendous amount of local attention, support, and funding, outraising more established major-party opponents. The advice was wrong—it was standard, partisan messaging, and **standard, partisan messaging is vulnerable.**

Within the current two-party paradigm, the most immediately profitable selling points are those most suited to play up the differences between red and blue. This is to say, if you as a candidate were to make a statement your opponent would agree with, or show support to a cause they would back, what reason does that give a voter to vote for you over them, or a donor to support you, and so forth?

It's not that mainstream candidates never bring up things like cost of living—they invoke such concerns plenty—but solutions only make practical sense to talk about if the Other Side would be trying to do the opposite. Polarizing issues, as a result, become the bread and butter of the parties, and divisive talking points are passed along from leadership down to ensure a distinct and consistent brand. The zero-sum dynamics also lead our major parties toward a tremendous amount of negative messaging—why try to win a voter over, after all, when you can simply tell them not to vote for the other guy?

All of this, however, combines to leave the parties' images mutually tarnished, and a significant number of key issues with real solutions untouched in messaging. These include frequent top priorities for voters such as infrastructure, mental health, and the aforementioned cost of living, the sort of "unsexy" subjects frowned upon by standard partisan messaging. **And because this predominant strategy so inhibits innovation, it leaves a growing hole in the market for dynamic thinkers to capitalize on.**

Whether they're discussed or not, we have massively complex problems in play, and how we solve them will have enormous consequences in the decades to come. How do we create better stability and resilience for our supply chains? How do we ready our industries and for AI and automation? How do we create real opportunity for our people in the face of global competition and the constantly evolving exploitation of economic power?

It goes far beyond economic issues. We must face conflict and chaos abroad, unpredictable weather and evolving pathogens, and the crises all of these carry. We must address the harms of social media and omnipresent flashing screens, and the poor mental health of generations stunted by so much technological and societal upheaval.

These aren't just unpleasant things to address through standard political thinking—they're impossible to. Finding real solutions demands a careful analysis of data, consideration of different perspectives and available tools, and a generous dose of foresight and planning. Addressing these issues, in a way that fosters genuine hope, demands dynamic and creative thinking, fresh ideas, and new voices—**precisely the sort of things that a healthier approach to discourse is best at producing.**

Moreover, if we embrace an open-minded and additive approach to conversation, then we will realize that the ideas we need to capitalize on these opportunities can come from anywhere. They can come from candidates for office and party leaders, from think tanks and nonprofits, from participants in town halls, public forums, and the broader discourse. **They can come from you.**

Give the People PUPPIES

Whether you have in mind a full-fledged policy proposal, an aspect to consider, or a way of discussing or presenting ideas, any contribution has the potential to have tremendous positive impact if it can fill some need. If you can understand where in the sphere of political thinking lies the greatest demand and the greatest opportunity to distinguish from standard partisan talking points, it becomes possible to identify how best to address it, and how you can contribute.

The question of what kind of messages best fit this mold is one I've spent a considerable amount of time contemplating. At Forward, I developed a tool for precisely this, and it remains one of my proudest accomplishments from my time there. It is not a recipe, but a set of seven criteria and guidelines which exemplify the fruits of healthy discourse and address demands and deficiencies in the sphere of political communication. And in great American tradition, it also makes use of a cute acronym.

Ladies and gentlemen, I give you PUPPIES.

To be effective in breaking through the noise, a message must first be **pertinent.** It must speak to societal need, to offer some pathway to societal benefit. In honing in on this, it is possible to take advantage of partisan overreliance on wedge issues or cultural hot buttons, and tap into a hunger for solutions in pressing matters like the cost of living, the health of our communities, and the state of our economic opportunity. Likewise, if your idea deals with something that is, on its surface, more niche or obscure—a piece of electoral reform, perhaps a particular tax incentive—it's essential to map out why it makes a difference in people's lives.

In the face of deep division and polarization, there is a greater need also for **unifying** messaging, built and refined to appeal to a wider audience. This goes beyond saying that some solution is for everyone—it's about utilizing tools for a common language and fostering a mindset of healthy discourse, to demonstrate that a message can resonate with a range of audiences. As it reaches the wider population and reaps the benefits of broader appeal, it can illustrate just how powerful a different approach can be.

Likewise, in the face of all the negativity that predominates our politics, there is an enormous need for something **positive.** This is not as easy as it sounds, but it is important to resist the temptation to tarnish, and to talk about not only dangers and excesses and error, but the good your idea can bring, and the hope it should inspire.

There is a need for ideas that are **pragmatic**, that acknowledge complex issues as complex issues, and showcase the attention to detail needed to create real solutions. Not only does this offer a signal of respect to voters and the public, but it is an argument in itself against simplistic and reductive ways of political thinking.

We also need **innovative** ideas, to bring something new and fresh to the table. Even if these are simply novel ways to present familiar arguments, this novelty demands attention and breaks the mold of tired and repetitive messaging from the machines. It utilizes the additive conversation, showcasing the dynamism that only a robust discourse produce.

Perhaps above all, there is a need for messaging that is **empowering**, capable of giving people a reason not only to hope but to see themselves as part of the hope. It should offer its audience a sense of agency not only over the democratic process, but over their own lives and how they should choose to live them. In a time of demoralization and despondency, it is the sort of resonance that has never been more needed, or more potent.

And finally, there is a need for messaging that is **self-aware,** that can exist not only as a hypothetical in the ether but as something ready to anticipate its reaction and response. This means a sense of realism and practicality, not only how some eventual policy would work, but also how it is going to find its audience and gain its necessary traction. When the predominant messaging feels increasingly disconnected, and when the powers-that-be rely on dismissing their challengers as delusional, this aspect of effective messaging is absolutely essential.

These are your PUPPIES—pertinent, unifying, positive, pragmatic, innovative, empowering, and self-aware. Not every message is going to check all seven, and not every message, even a great one, can. But a movement that embraces these virtues is not only one we should want to see succeed—it is also well-positioned to do precisely that.

In Search of Pudding, for Proof Purposes

I've come so far while trying to leave my personal opinions on issues out of this text, and I'd like to think I've been reasonably successful in doing so. Those opinions were never the point, and they would have limited my audience and distracted from what was. It would be a shame to break the streak now and share a personal take on something like abortion, but that's exactly what I'm going to do.

It's not that the topic is so personally dear to me—no more than anyone else. It's not that I'm so sure in my opinion—it's just my opinion, and it's not a particularly deeply researched one. However, I do believe it is worth highlighting to demonstrate the possibilities that flow from this kind of political thinking, and where its greatest potential may lie. So, if you will, bear with me.

In short, I don't see any clear evidence that outlawing abortions would be an effective way to reduce abortions when under-the-table and extralegal methods (which would be far more accessible with modern pharmaceutical technology) are taken into account. Statewide or localized bans seem likely to have limited effectiveness for all but the poorest and most vulnerable populations, as others seeking the services would likely be able to access them elsewhere.

I also believe, however, that we have more shared sentiment than we realize on wanting to reduce the situations that would lead one to potentially decide to have an abortion—even for those who have no moral opposition to it, it can be a potentially traumatic experience for those who undergo it. As such, for both those focused on reducing and minimizing the abortions, and for those focused on ensuring safe and legal access, the best solution would seem to be federally codified legality, combined with an initiative to reduce the number of unwanted pregnancies and abortions occurring (which can only be effectively tracked if they're legal) through effective sex education, financial resources and support for young mothers and the expecting, safe access to contraception, and a range of other data-supported programs.

I don't expect everyone to agree with my take—creating a consensus isn't my goal, and even I don't believe the idea is fully fleshed out. But I hope this example can illustrate that collaborative problem-solving doesn't have to mean compromises and sacrifices, that it is capable of producing more sustainable and better outcomes for many across the political spectrum.

Put more simply, my point is not to say this is some perfect policy, but that it is an example of trying to gear seemingly opposite perspectives toward a common goal. If you can make the case, through this idea or any other, that people would be better represented in the long term by dynamic problem solvers than by common partisans who claim to share their values, then there is no compromise they need to worry about, and it becomes abundantly clear why a healthier discourse is something we should all be striving toward.

Too often, we assume that the path to being better heard is fighting harder and yelling louder. We can shatter that assumption, and prove the strength of better discourse, through our successes, from our personal growth and deeper understanding of ourselves, to more fruitful and positive interactions with friends and loved ones, to political breakthroughs and policy ideas better than any I could have ever conceived.

The onus will be upon us, then, to demonstrate that a leader who empowers the people to speak and engage in healthy conversation will represent their interests and defend their rights better than any who claims to speak for them. If we can do that, the world will take notice.

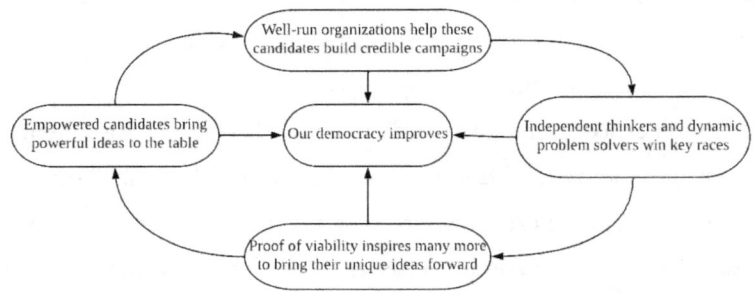

---

1. "Voter Turnout in American Elections since 2000." *States United Democracy Center*, 25 July 2024

2. BROWNSTEIN, RONALD. "Both Parties Favored Perot, Exit Poll Shows : Presidency: The Texan Would Have Won Democratic and GOP Races I." Los Angeles Times, 3 June 1992

Conclusion

The Case Against Optimism

I hope that I have shown here that a healthy discourse and a constructive, problem-solving mindset can change our world for the better. **Please, do not take this to mean that they will.**

There are, of course, many variables and unknowns in play. World events may shift thinking, force actions, or irreparably change our situation. Other political thinkers will have their own approaches they push forward, which may resonate with the public. Media coverage may affect what messages spread and where.

Regardless of any of this, though, a broad and self-certain optimism, just like a broad and self-certain pessimism, would make us out to be passive observers to the inevitable. Yes, there will be factors beyond our control, but we can still have an impact. What each one of us does—what you do—matters.

We can make a difference through our political efforts and our contributions, and not just the monetary ones. Showing what can work and what can resonate can call people to action and make them feel a part of the democratic process in a way they have not before.

We can make a difference through the conversations we have with others, through the ways we express our ideas and engage with differing perspectives, and even through our personal growth in confidence and self-awareness. By showcasing a healthier political mindset, we can challenge others' assumptions and open their minds as never before.

> The onus is upon us to demonstrate
> that a leader who empowers the people to
> speak and engage in healthy conversation will
> represent their interests and defend their rights
> better than any who claims to speak for them.
> If we can do that, the world will take notice.

Every impact reverberates in more ways than we realize. Add up enough of them, and you have on your hands a wave of real societal change, capable of shifting incentives and making new endeavors to improve our democracy possible.

Looking at the road ahead, I think back again to the loss of my father in my formative years. It was an experience that instilled in me the importance of not taking anything for granted, but alongside this sometimes fearful sense of uncertainty came a deeper appreciation for all the good we can do and achieve. **It is because I am not an optimist, and because I hold no great sense of certainty about the future, that I can rejoice as much as I do when both personal and societal progress is made, because I understand it's not inevitable.**

History repeats itself, yes, until it doesn't, until new patterns emerge and defy what we know and expect. Will this be the moment when we can break through the noise and the cultural chaos to rethink and redefine what politics can be in the modern era?

To be honest, I'm not sure. But I will try my darndest to have something to say about it. And I hope you do, too.

Acknowledgements

This is a book about the virtues and benefits of working together, and it would not have been possible without those friends by my side to challenge me, to guide me, and to offer their invaluable perspectives along the way. To Kimberly, to Chris, to Dan, and to so many more, thank you. And to all of those whose experience I have leaned on through my political and writing journeys—to Matt, to Danielle, to Kim (different Kim), and to all of the former elected leaders and political organizers who lent me their time and attention—thank you.

I would also not be in this position were it not for the love and support of my family. Thank you to my amazing wife, whose aesthetic sensibility I have leaned on greatly, in no small part because of my complete lack thereof. Thank you to my grandparents, who helped so much to raise me and shape the person I am today. I will not be thanking my mother here, as I have already given her credit several times throughout this text for the values she helped to instill in me, and I don't want it getting to her head.

Lastly, the message that I share here is only as powerful as my readers make it. So to all of you, for your time and attention, for opening your minds for what I have to offer, from the bottom of my heart, thank you.

www.ingramcontent.com/pod-product-compliance
Lightning Source LLC
Chambersburg PA
CBHW070814120626
46556CB00002B/503